DUSTIN

HOFFMAN

THE CLASSIC

PERFORMANCES

By Chris Wade

Dustin Hoffman: The Classic Performances

by Chris Wade

Wisdom Twins Books, 2019

wisdomtwinsbooks.weebly.com

DUSTIN HOFFMAN

THE CLASSIC PERFORMANCES

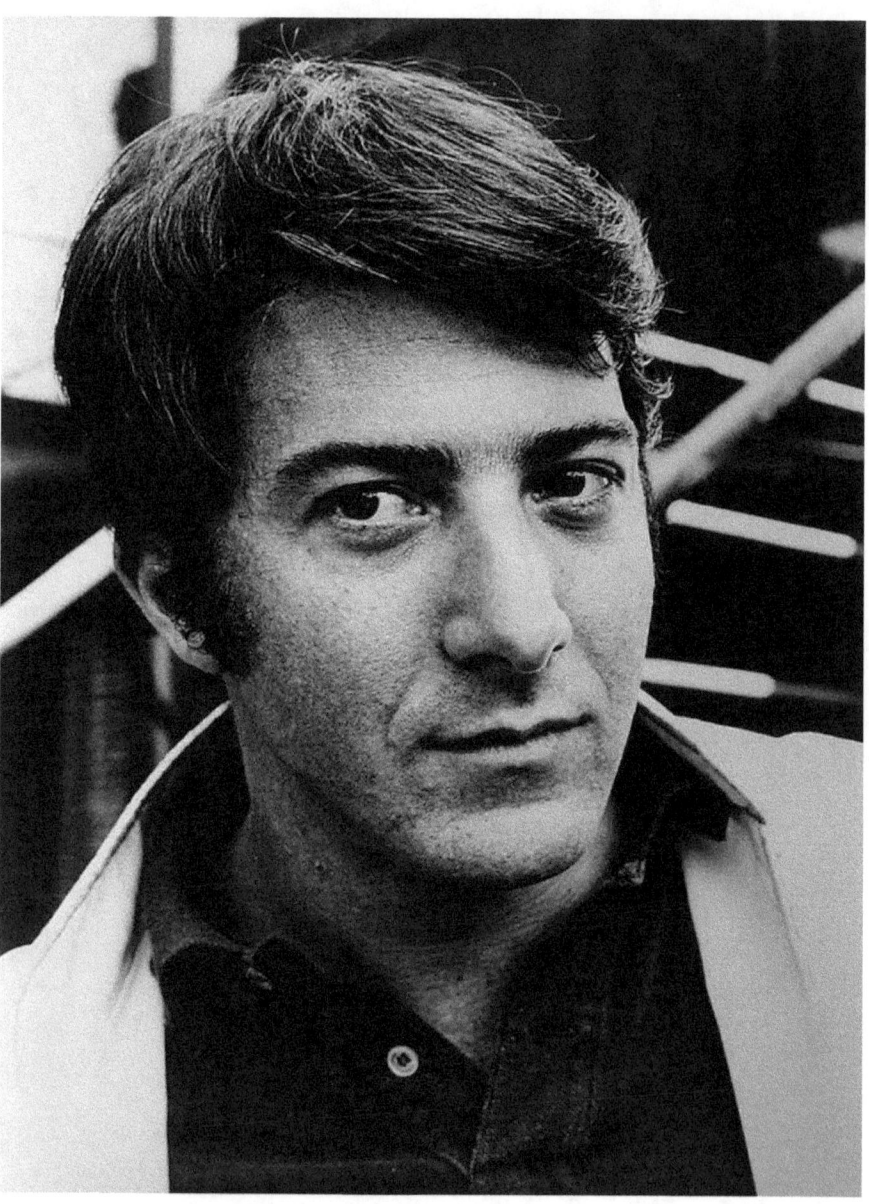

CONTENTS

The Hoffman Paradox: The Character Actor Turned Leading Man

"Are You Here For An Affair? - Benjamin Braddock, The Graduate
and Dustin Hoffman As Iconic Outsider

"What was the Baby Picture?" - Dustin Hoffman as Ratso Rizzo

"I Have A Horse and Four Wives." - Dustin Hoffman in Little Big Man

The "Right" Choice:
The Overlooked Films of Dustin Hoffman in the 1970s

"I Don't Know My Way Home..."
Hoffman Becomes A Peckinpah Man in Straw Dogs

"I Say A Lot of Words..." - Dustin Hoffman As Lenny Bruce

"Is it Safe?" - Dustin Hoffman as the Marathon Man

The Value of Authenticity:
Dustin Hoffman in Kramer Vs Kramer and Tootsie

Was It Really So Bad?
The Case for Ishtar, Legendary Box Office Bomb

"I'm An Excellent Driver..."

Dustin Hoffman As Raymond Babbit in Rain Man

The Curious Nineties: A Decade of Ups and Downs

Last Chance Hoffman: Dustin Hoffman in Last Chance Harvey

About Chris Wade

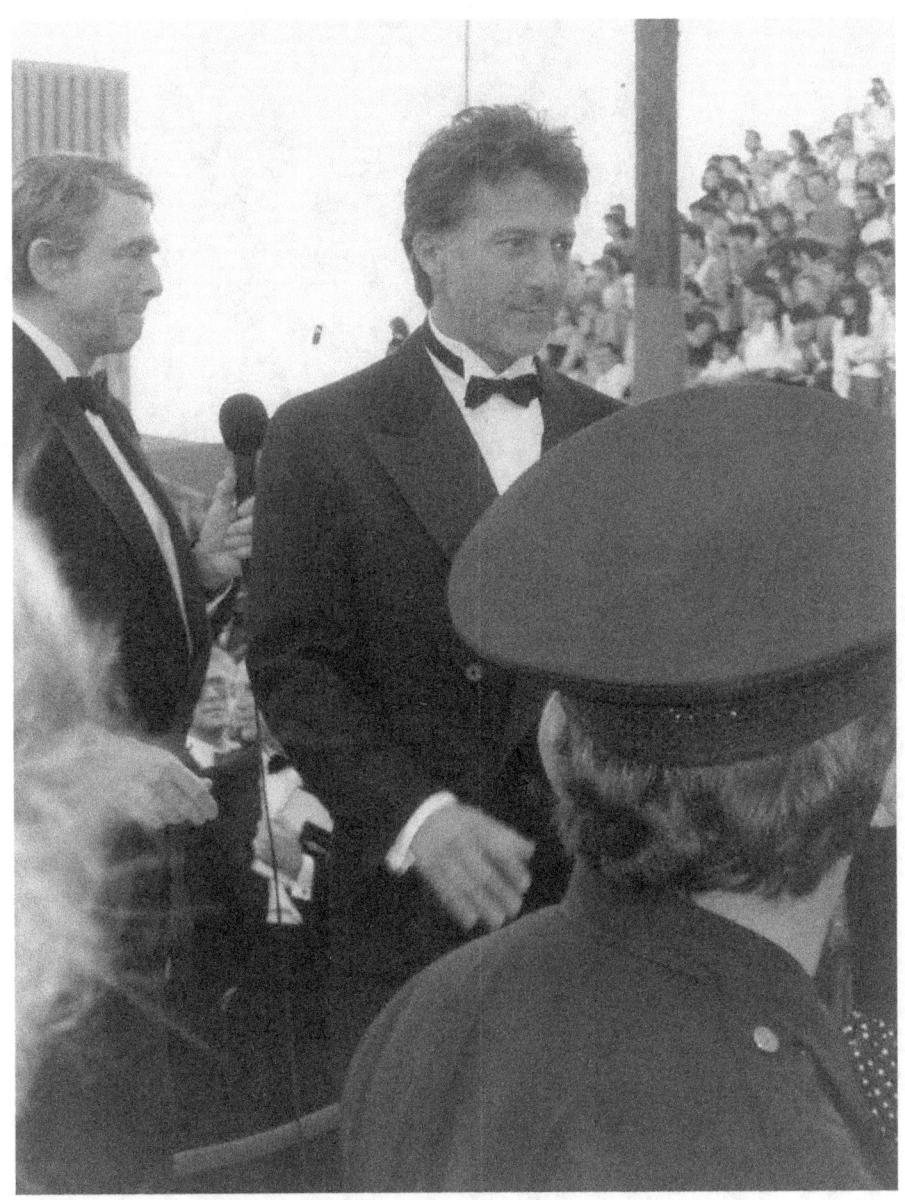

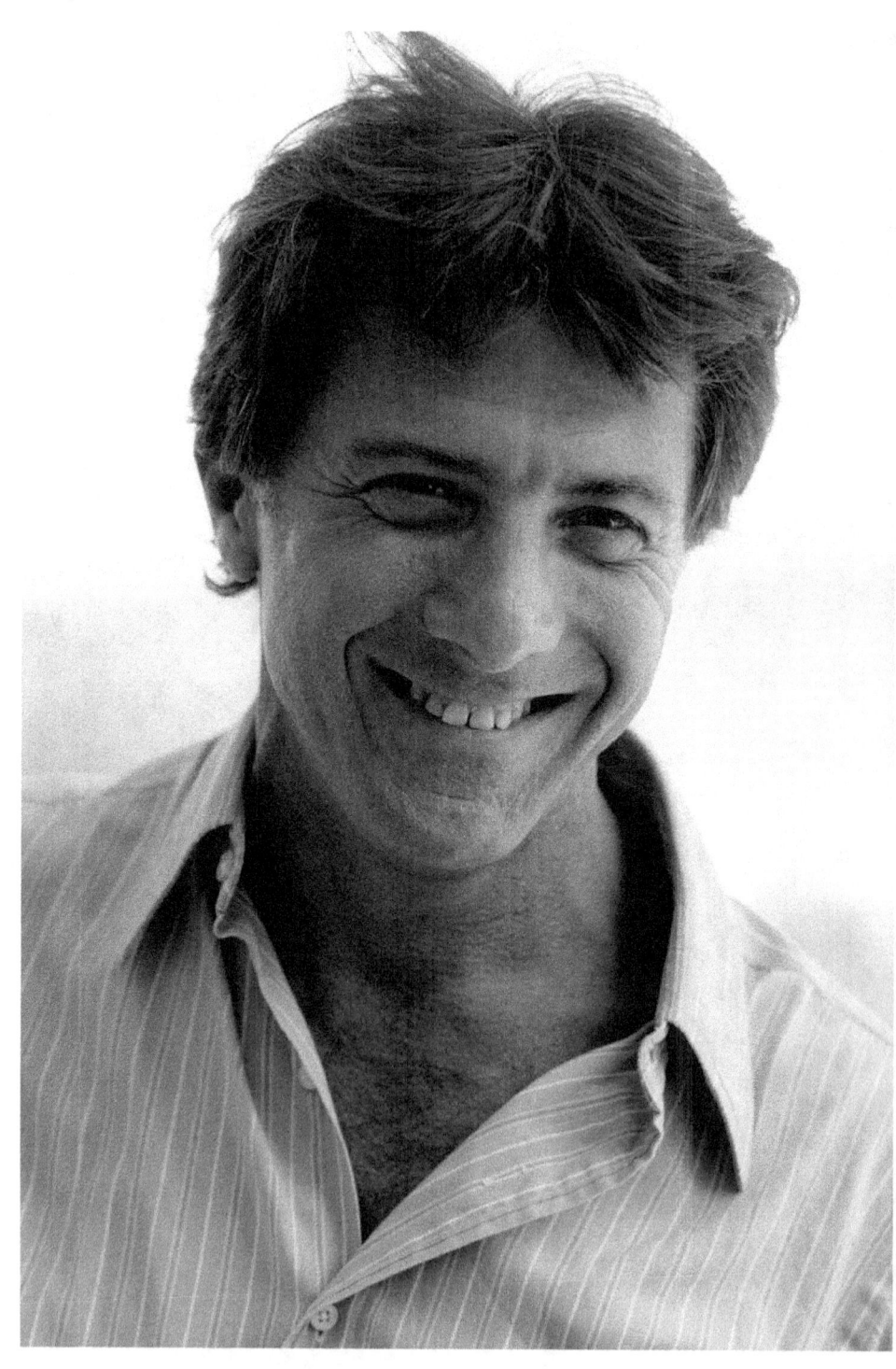

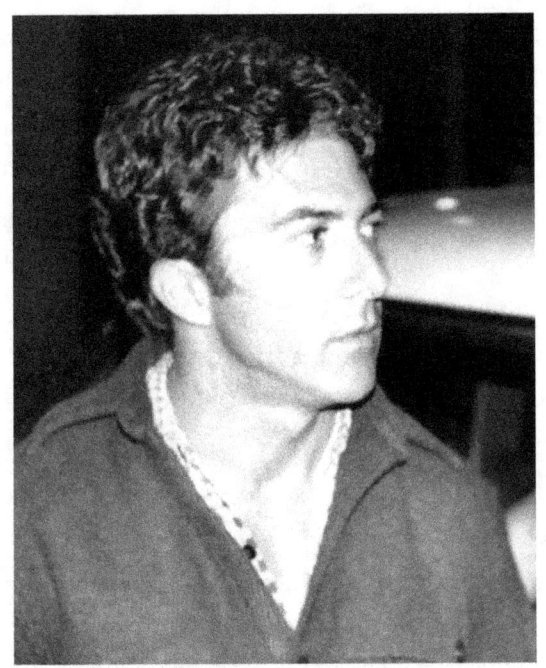

The Hoffman Paradox

The Character Actor Turned Leading Man

Of that remarkable generation of actors to emerge during the so called New Hollywood boom of the late sixties and early to mid seventies, few made as many memorable and important movies, and gave as many breathtaking performances, as Dustin Hoffman. Though many would now say the era belonged to such angry males as Al Pacino, Robert De Niro and Jack Nicholson, it was in fact Dustin who was the first out of these fine performers to find success, when he hit the screens and redefined what a movie lead could look like, and indeed *be*, with his marvellous turn as the alienated and disenchanted Benjamin Braddock in Mike Nichols' The Graduate, released in 1967.

Hoffman had been working on the stage for years until his unexpected big break came and turned thirty when the film was released at the back end of the year, ancient by Hollywood standards. But this film arrived at the right point, and didn't just change Hoffman's life, but the whole of the film industry. The anti hero was born, and in the wake of The Graduate, and Hoffman's newfound stardom, Hollywood loosened its bullets and let down the impenetrable gates, welcoming in a host of maverick directors and unconventional stars to get them back in touch with their audience, who had largely abandoned the movies for the allure of rock and pop. This does over generalise a whole era somewhat, but the New Hollywood craze does explain why someone like Hoffman, so short and awkward in The Graduate, a role meant for a "Robert Redford type", could break into leading man status so unexpectedly.,

With The Graduate becoming a social phenomenon in itself, Hoffman, whether he wanted this or not, was transformed into a kind of poster boy for a generation at odds with their elders, in search of an idol who could project their own disillusionment and make some sense of their feelings. The problem was of course that Hoffman was a good ten years older than the character he played in The Graduate, and though he appreciated his fame and popularity, not to mention the female attention he was receiving as the newest and least likely sex symbol of the big screen, he wasn't ready to be the saviour of an alienated youth. Disappointing his needy fans further, Hoffman took a year to decide on his next role, and rather than going for a hip choice in a similar vein to The Graduate and capitalising on his cool image, he went in the complete opposite direction by portraying the homeless outsider turned reluctant pimp, Rico "Ratso" Rizzo in John

Schlesinger's masterpiece, Midnight Cowboy, which won Best Picture at the Oscars in 1969. The film was a brave move and a complete transformation for Hoffman. Wisely, from the word go he ensured his audience he was not a predictable leading man, but a daring character actor, willing to take risks few others would dare to.

These two films were enough to make Hoffman a legend forever, but they could not have been further from each other in almost every way. The only area where Benjamin and Ratso were similar though, vitally it seems, is that they were both outsiders; Benjamin an awkward social outcast, Ratso a seedy "invisible man", existing on the parameters of society but reaching out for a connection. Hoffman portrayed both men with a masterly approach that went way beyond his years. It was, of course, down to the experience he'd garnered both on the stage and in life itself.

He was born in August of 1937 in Los Angeles, the son of Harry Hoffman, a movie props man turned furniture salesman, and Lillian. Though Jewish, his childhood was not religious in any way. After graduating school, originally planning to become a classical pianist, he took up acting in college. Not gifted in music, he gave up the piano and focused on performing, which became his creative outlet. Doing odd jobs while failing to win acting work, he moved to New York with his friend Gene Hackman, and the pair moved in with another rising actor, a certain Robert Duvall. Though still struggling, he was excited by the Big Apple. He later remembered getting off the bus and immediately seeing someone pissing against a car. "I thought: yes, I'm not in a plastic environment any more," Hoffman told the Guardian recently.

Hoffman also explained the early prejudices that were present during his auditions for roles. "There were two papers, Backstage and Showbiz, you got to try to get a job," he said. "It would list the parts available, and they would say: Leading men, leading women, leading juveniles, leading ingénues; character leading men, character ingénues, character juveniles – that was the funny-looking Semitic guy. That meant you weren't good-looking, and good-looking meant white Anglo-Saxon protestant."

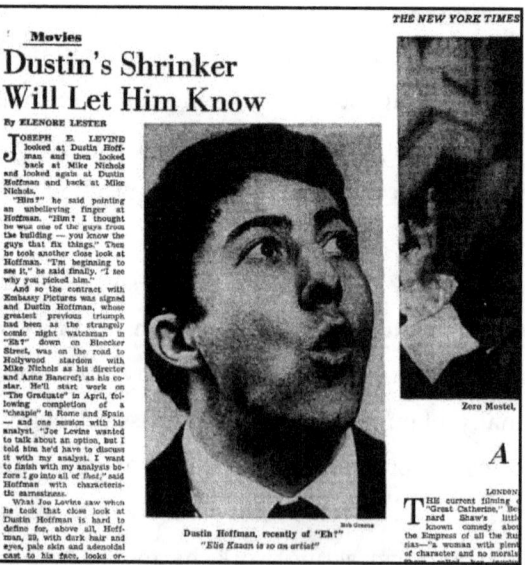

An early press cutting of Hoffman on stage in the hit play Eh?

Hoffman initially earned acclaim on stage, most notably in the play Eh?, and then in Harry, Noon and Night, in which he played a German Nazi Homosexual with a limp and a hump. "I read that," Hoffman recalled, "and said: That's the part for me!"

This led to The Graduate and the unlikely chance of a lifetime. "Nichols chose to give this short, funny-looking Jewish guy the role usually reserved for a tall, handsome protestant," he later said. It may have been bold of Nichols to cast him, but he wouldn't have done it if Hoffman didn't have the talent. It was a life changing role, earning him award nominations from every corner. The fact he took so long to mull over his next film proved that success hadn't warped his sense of values.

Hoffman found fame perplexing. "Yes, it was different to be walking down Fifth Avenue with a girl with beautiful breasts come up to you and say, Sign me," he said, "that did not happen before. The truth of it is that I got a lot of crappy parts offered to me and I didn't want to make movies any more; I wanted to go back to the theatre."

Hoffman performed on Broadway in the musical Jimmy Shine before deciding to work with Schlesinger. In truth, his choice to play Ratso was about more than proving his versatility. After all, he felt an affinity with the part. "I was closer to Ratso Rizzo when I was going to school," he recalled, "that's what I felt like. I was an outsider, on the periphery looking in. And when I came to New York I did all those odd jobs, and if you're cleaning toilets for a living you're not that far from being Ratso so it wasn't that difficult a part."

Midnight Cowboy was released alongside another film. Often leapt over in retrospective looks at Hoffman's career, John and Mary stands in the period between the release and huge successes of Midnight Cowboy and Arthur Penn's Little Big Man (1970), and perhaps for that reason is neglected these days. Directed by the then fashionable filmmaker Peter Yates (who had made Bullitt the year before), the concept of John and Mary is very typical of its time, but features the kind of plot device that seemed rather dated within only a decade or so. Still, though not covered in detail in the main chapters of this book, it does deserve singling out as an example that young Hoffman did make a conventional picture.

It begins on the morning after John (Dustin Hoffman) and Mary (Mia Farrow) meet in a bar, in bed after their night together. The film goes through their first conversation, which was on the topic of a Jean Luc Godard movie (again, very typical of the time), and their breakfast meal, over which they get to know one another. There are also frequent flashbacks to their previous relationships, which are conventionally presented to the viewer (unlike the flashbacks in Midnight Cowboy). The performances are good of course, and considering how fresh and vital Farrow and Hoffman were at the time, there is little wonder that they do so well in these potentially clichéd circumstances. Again, Hoffman's John could not have been further from the recent Ratso; indeed, to think the same man could play such different men within a few months is a testament to his abilities.

It seems rather unfair to compare Hoffman's John and Mary role with his earlier Ratso, because Midnight Cowboy gave him so many opportunities to shine. Limping, coughing and subtly winning our sympathy despite playing an unsavoury character, Ratso is a showy role delivered in a theatrical manner but made to fit the confinements of cinema. John in John and Mary is more of a realistic, straight forward part, and Hoffman is clearly using more of his own physicality to portray this naturalistic character. He does just enough to bring the part to life. That said, Hoffman actually won a BAFTA for his performance and was nominated for a Golden Globe. He was proving, two years on from The Graduate, that he was a serious talent with a future ahead of him. He was also a leading man, whether he wanted to admit it or not.

Following this trio of starring vehicles, he continued to go into ever more unexpected directions. In 1970 he donned heavy make up to play the 121 year old Jack Crabb in Little Big Man, a role which further illustrated his remarkable range. What could have been a ludicrous cartoon strip of a film and performance was elevated, mostly, by Hoffman's multi layered, entertaining and ultimately brilliant portrayal of a man we see from his teens to his triple figures.

The 1970s were just as fruitful as the latter part of the 1960s. There were mainstream hits like Papillon (1973), but more controversial fare, such as Sam Peckinpah's Straw Dogs (1971) and Bob Fosse's Lenny (1974), which earned Hoffman another Oscar nomination for his striking portrayal of doomed comic Lenny Bruce. Though he came to the world's attention in the sixties, it was the seventies that made Hoffman the reliable screen actor he became. Other films included the action thriller Marathon Man (1976), which proved Hoffman could carry a more conventional type of film, in this case a commercial thriller. (Covered later in the book.)

One of the most celebrated films of Hoffman's career came the same year with All the President's Men, Alan J Pakula's thrilling retelling of the Watergate scandal. As Woodward and Bernstein, Robert Redford and Dustin Hoffman delivered two of the most iconic characterisations of the decade. There is the sense that Woodward and Bernstein/Redford and Hoffman are the same man, and the two actors ensured this would be the case by overlapping one another during scenes, sharing dialogue to suggest that the two hot shot reporters are so intensely together in solving this case that they know they are stronger as a single unit. Jason Robards, who won an Oscar for his role as the Washington Post's editor, sums this up perfectly by repeatedly calling out "Woodstein!"

Of course we have Redford himself to thank for this production, who bought the book rights immediately upon publication, for a whopping $450,000. Hoffman was not the first choice for Bernstein. Redford first thought of Al Pacino, and one can certainly imagine him in the part. The frantic energy he brought to the likes of Serpico and Dog Day Afternoon makes him a believable candidate for the hurried pace of All the President's Men, but Pacino lacked that almost scholarly authority that Hoffman was able to embody. Yes Hoffman could be frantic and nervy, but there was control behind it, whereas Pacino, when playing a more frenzied, wound up character, seemed like he could explode at any minute. The key to Hoffman's Bernstein is the combination of journalistic excitement and solid logic, the investigator tripping over himself to get to the truth, but also tightly wound enough to deliver the goods. These days it's hard to imagine anyone but Hoffman standing beside Redford in the film.

Redford and Hoffman really do transform into the duo before our eyes. Ever the method actor, Hoffman (and Redford of course) saw fit to visit the Washington Post offices time and time again, getting a feel for the atmosphere, the mood and the pace of a day in the office. In order to tune himself into that almost chaotic world, papers flying back and forth, feet scurrying on carpeted floors with a hot scoop, Hoffman had to absorb the vibes, the sense of urgency running through the corridors and across the vast office spaces.

These hits aside, Hoffman took some odd choices in the 1970s, from Alfredo, Alfredo and Who is Harry Kellerman and Why is He

Saying Those Terrible Things About Me?, to Agatha and the underrated crime thriller Straight Time. There were also roaring successes too. Kramer vs. Kramer, his last film of the decade, was a gripping tale of divorce. It not only won Best Picture at the Oscars, it also bagged Hoffman his first Academy Award for Best Actor.

The eighties were not as hectic as far as film work went, though at either side of 1987's commercially disappointing but rather underrated Ishtar, he did set screens alight in Tootsie (1982) and the wonderful Rain Man (1988) where he played the autistic Raymond Babbit and bagged another Oscar, deservedly I might add. His Babbit remains one of cinema's most memorable and brilliantly observed performances, another example of Hoffman disappearing before our eyes and becoming the character. It was a different type of film acting, half method, half something else - otherworldly, almost spiritual. He also returned to the stage, triumphantly, playing Willy Loman in the brilliant Death of a Salesman, which was filmed as a TV movie in 1985. He won an Emmy and a Golden Globe for the performance, which for me is one of his finest.

Though it's arguable whether Hoffman ever reached these kind of heights again, he continued to appear in entertaining and often brilliant films; Wag the Dog (1997) for instance earned him another Oscar nomination, and he was excellent in minor films like Mad City (also 1997) and David Mamet's American Buffalo (1996), for my money his finest performance of the past thirty years.

As this book focuses on classic Hoffman performances however, one point I must raise is how seldom Hoffman has matched his classic work in the new millennium. He'd enjoyed a fruitful decade in the 90s and scaled personal heights as far as film performance went.

After his brief cameo in the Luc Besson Joan of Arc movie in 1999, he took three years off the screen before signing up for another movie, the unsuccessful Moonlight Mile, released in 2002. An underrated gem, it remains one of his best works in the past twenty or so years. Based on true events in the life of writer and director Brad Silberling, centring on a young man (played by Jake Gyllenhall) who befriends his girlfriend's parents (Dustin Hoffman and Susan Sarandon) after she is murdered. The movie itself is rather touching, slight and benefits greatly from the finely tuned performances. It received good reviews and Hoffman in particular deservedly got singled out for his work. It's one of his quieter roles and I personally found some of his softer moments very moving. Some reviewers, Roger Ebert included, couldn't help but notice Hoffman's character was called Benjamin, like the confused youth in The Graduate. Funnily enough though, he is more Death of a Salesman than The Graduate. It's a role that wouldn't necessarily jump out as a career highlight, but it does show how subtle he can be.

Hoffman also shone bright, though in a completely different manner, in James Foley's tense thriller Confidence. At his most menacing, he plays a Los Angeles crime lord known as The King, oozing villainy and controlled nastiness. The movie itself was rather uneven, but Dustin's restrained effort, a man ready to explode out of his calm exterior into explosive violence at any minute, was a master class in subtlety. Roger Ebert, finding the film lacking, was impressed by Dustin's work, writing, "Dustin Hoffman's performance as the King is the best thing in the movie--indeed, the only element that comes to life on the screen, screen, instead of in a twice-told tale. The King runs a strip club as a front, launders money for the mob, and suffers from Attention Deficit Disorder--or, as he meticulously specifies, "Attention Deficit Hyperactivity Disorder." To control his condition, he takes pills that slow him way down. Feel my heart, he says to one of the strippers in his club, to prove that it is hardly beating. Hoffman, chewing gum, wearing a beard and glasses, looks like the gnome from hell, and fast-talks his way into a brilliant supporting performance. So brilliant, I couldn't help wondering how much energy the film would have gained if Hoffman, say, had played the lead instead of (Edward) Burns. With Hoffman, you look at him and try to figure out what he's thinking."

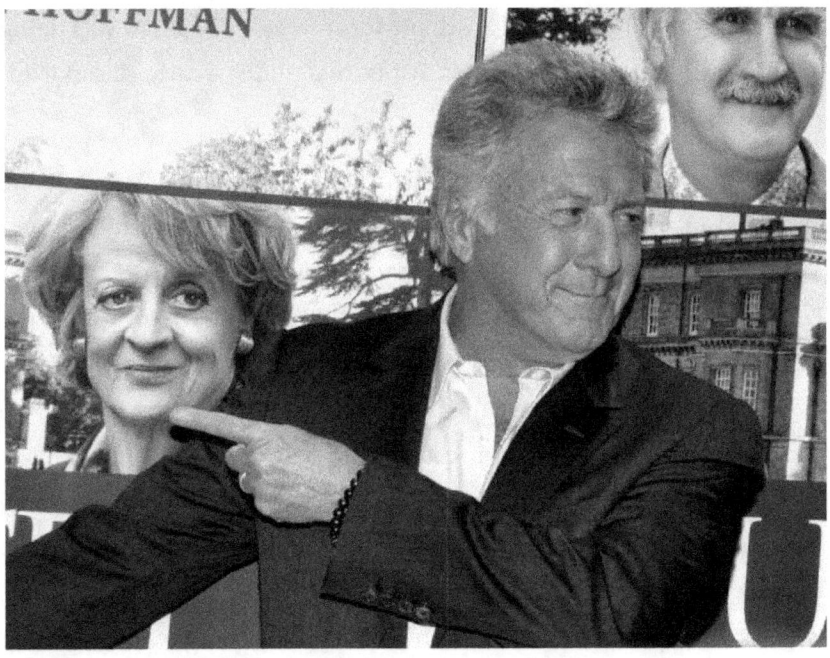

The problem with assessing one man's work within a motion picture is that he is but one molecule within a complete structure. A film like Confidence, messy and overly familiar at times, does not truly warrant a performance of such depth. And as this is no study of humanity that the viewer can really gain anything from (it should be noted that Hoffman's earlier work, or the best of it, always seemed like a learning curve for both Hoffman and the viewer), Confidence feels like an empty vessel, barely entertaining except when Dustin creeps on to the screen.

In this period Hoffman was providing his solid presence to movies that were far from inspiring, though completely adequate in terms of what they were trying to achieve. His role in Gary Fleder's Runaway Jury was, again, nicely played, but nothing in the film makes it stand out and all these years on it's all but forgotten. If Hoffman was doing good work, it was too often in films that didn't really deserve his presence.

Yet he was also busiest he had ever been. In 2004 alone he appeared in four movies. The first was a sequel to one of the biggest hits of the period, Meet the Parents. This one, entitled Meet the Fockers, moved things on from the 2000 Jay Roach original, the highly original and genuinely well made Meet the Parents. For better or worse, this tired follow up involved the Burns clan (led by the grouchy Robert De Niro) meeting the Fockers, his son in law's parents. Dustin Hoffman is the relaxed, emotional and slightly eccentric father, a "Mr Mom" and proud of it. He wears his heart on his sleeve and this bugs Jack no end. Greg's mother, Barbra Streisand, is a sex therapist and starts to rub Jack up the wrong way by getting nosey regarding his sex life. Things eventually turn sour when the two families clash on a whole number of issues, but eventually reach a kind of truce.

But there is an issue here which needs focusing on, especially as this is a book on Hoffman's performances. As such a huge admirer of the man's work since my childhood, it's odd to admit that I not only dislike his character and performance in Fockers, but that it irritates me profusely. Often referred to as comic marmite in reviews, I know which side I fall on; it's my least favourite Hoffman character. It's sad to admit that, yes, Hoffman is annoying in Meet the Fockers, and one definitely tires of his supposedly hilarious antics by the end of this unmercifully long film. He seems to be trying very hard to be kooky, but in my view it falls flat.

Roger Ebert, a man who had observed Hoffman's career on film from the start, liked Hoffman's work, even if he found the film so-so and uninspiring: "Streisand and Hoffman create characters who are, under the circumstances, not only likable but actually sort of believable. Yet even if you loved Meet the Parents, you will only sorta kinda like Meet the Fockers."

A smart man, Hoffman was aware that his performances were not as rigidly dedicated as they once had been. "But I never argue with people, even friends, who say: Oh, you just walked through Meet the Fockers. Or: Oh, you were just yourself in Last Chance Harvey, you just walked through that! The truth is that every movie is difficult. You shoot out of sequence. You shoot only two or three pages a day. You're always making choices."

Ploughing on ahead, Hoffman took notable roles in a mixed bag of movies. He was good in Stranger Than Fiction (2006) and I Heart Huckabees (2004), but the films themselves were not led by his performances. It's a cliché to say they don't make movies like they once did, but one can say with truthfulness that Hoffman doesn't make movies like he used to, and that's perhaps because he's not as intensely dedicated to his craft as he once was. It's also down to his age and the kind of roles he is being offered.

Hoffman said as much in a 2008 interview: "After The Graduate, suddenly the best parts were offered to me. This goes on for decades and then you wake up one morning and you're not being offered leads any more. You're being offered supports. Then you're reading the lead and thinking: This is great – but you remember you're too old for it... and if you don't look in the mirror, they do. I prefer to play a lead because you can make it three-dimensional, but what's wonderful is that you have this enormous elephant taken off your chest (in supporting roles). You're not carrying the movie. It's not your responsibility.'

These days, now over 80, Hoffman continues to work, though he has been quieter in the past couple of years and has tended to lean more towards animated features than anything requiring physical demand. The fact he is not making important films now is not really his fault. As he admits, the roles are not being offered and those films, like Kramer vs. Kramer and Rain Man, are simply not being made in the mainstream. And those who say he doesn't care as much about his craft anymore must ask themselves a question - can one really care as much about Kung Fu Panda (which Hoffman has a recurring voice role in) as Midnight Cowboy?

Hoffman is also aware that the industry has changed. He clearly does not want to be a part of the sci-fi/superhero world, so he chooses films that fall outside popularity. "There's a temporariness if they're not Star Wars or things of that ilk. What do they call all those TV formats now? Streaming? That's where we're going. We're on the way out. I've made a couple of films recently that haven't been able to get distribution or that have really had a hard time. One, The Program, Stephen Frears directed it about Lance Armstrong and, my God, that's been finished for over a year and they're having trouble getting distribution – and it's a well-done film. It's tough."

On the other side of this rather negative train of thought, however, is the fact that Dustin finally overcame his fear of directing a film of his own when he made his well received Quartet, perhaps the most important film for him personally in the past twenty years. But as he did not act in the film, it is not covered in this book. Still, the movie proves he is still up for fresh challenges.

Even if he does not make another great movie, Dustin Hoffman will be remembered forever as one of the great American screen actors, someone who changed the way things were, who was made an icon by embodying the antithesis of everything Hollywood had once encouraged its leading men to be. Those classics performances, many discussed in the text to follow, have ensured his place in film legend.

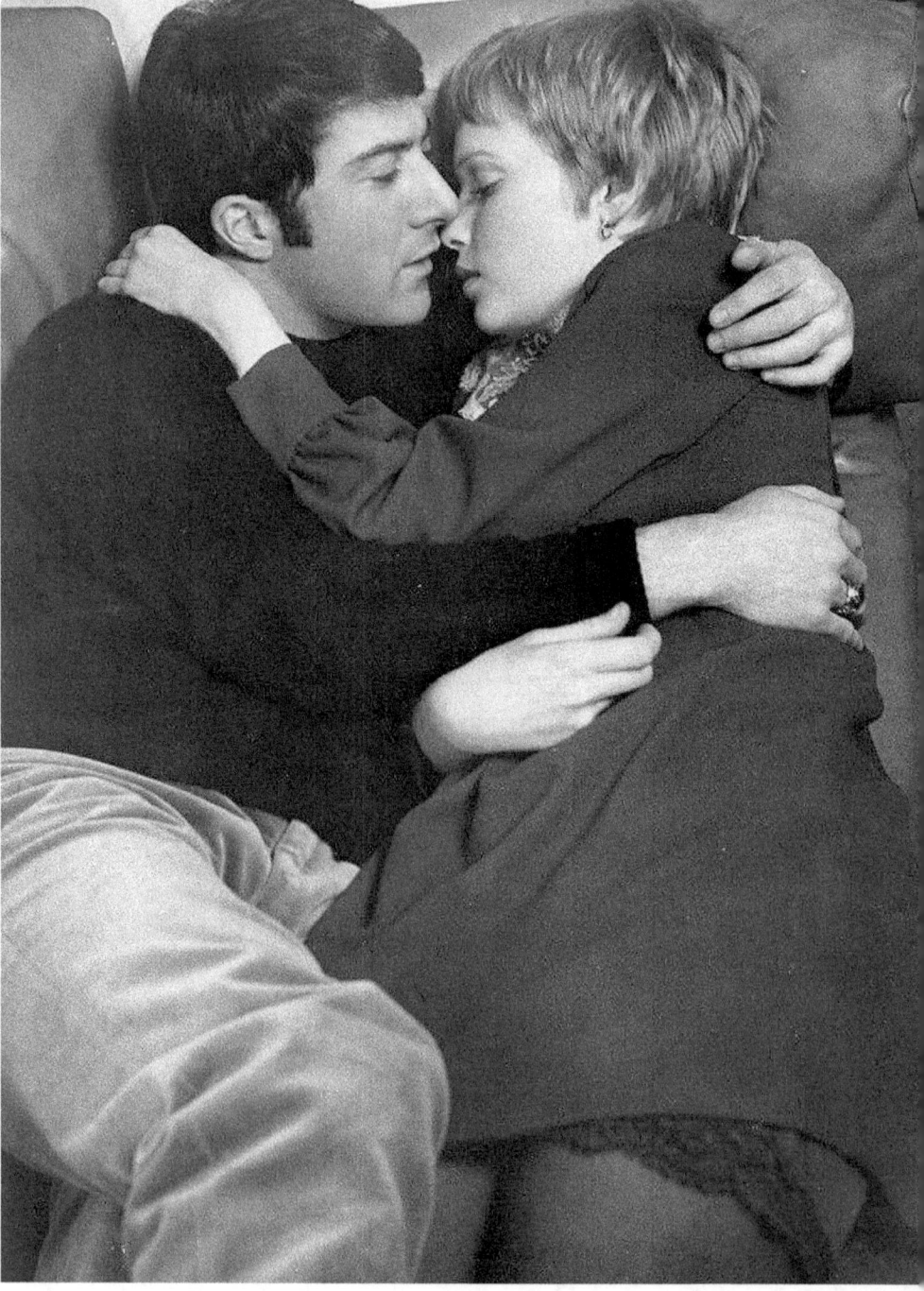

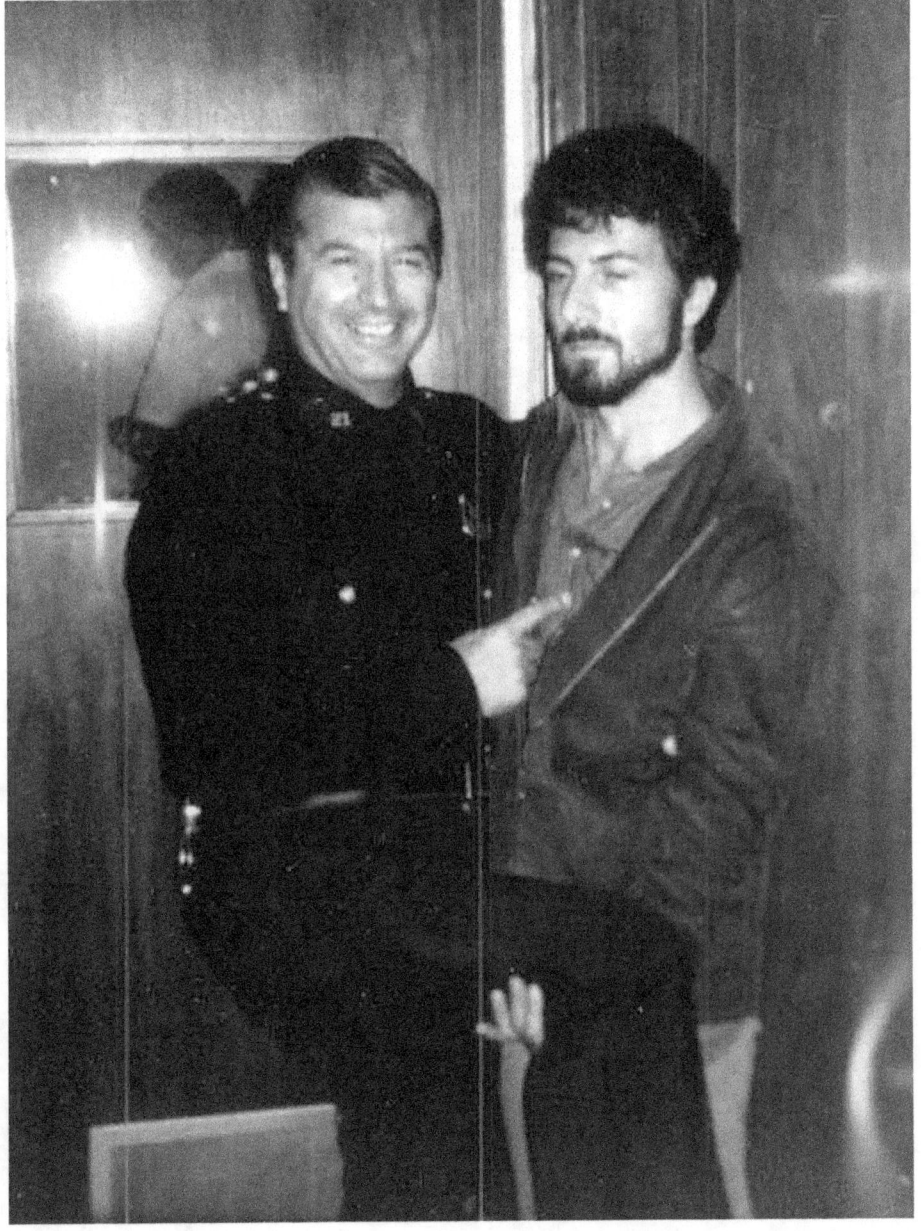

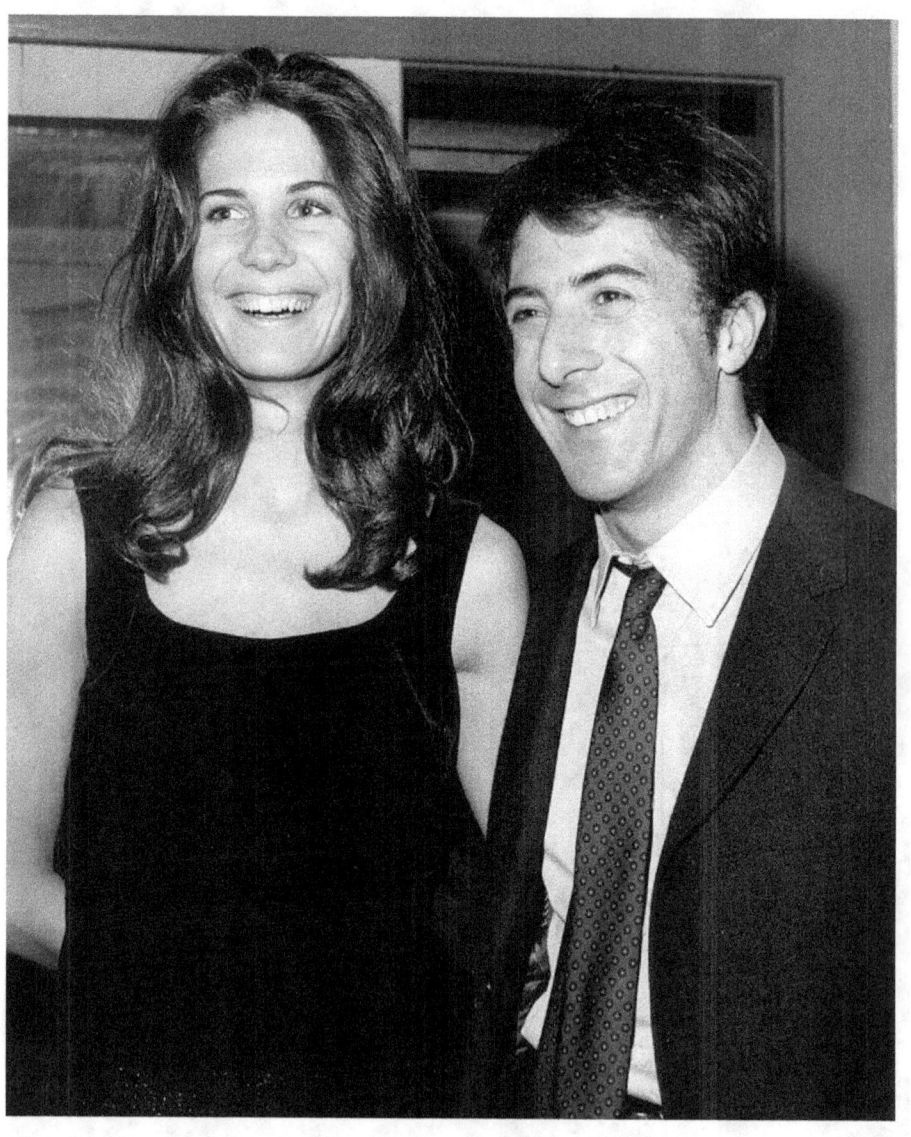

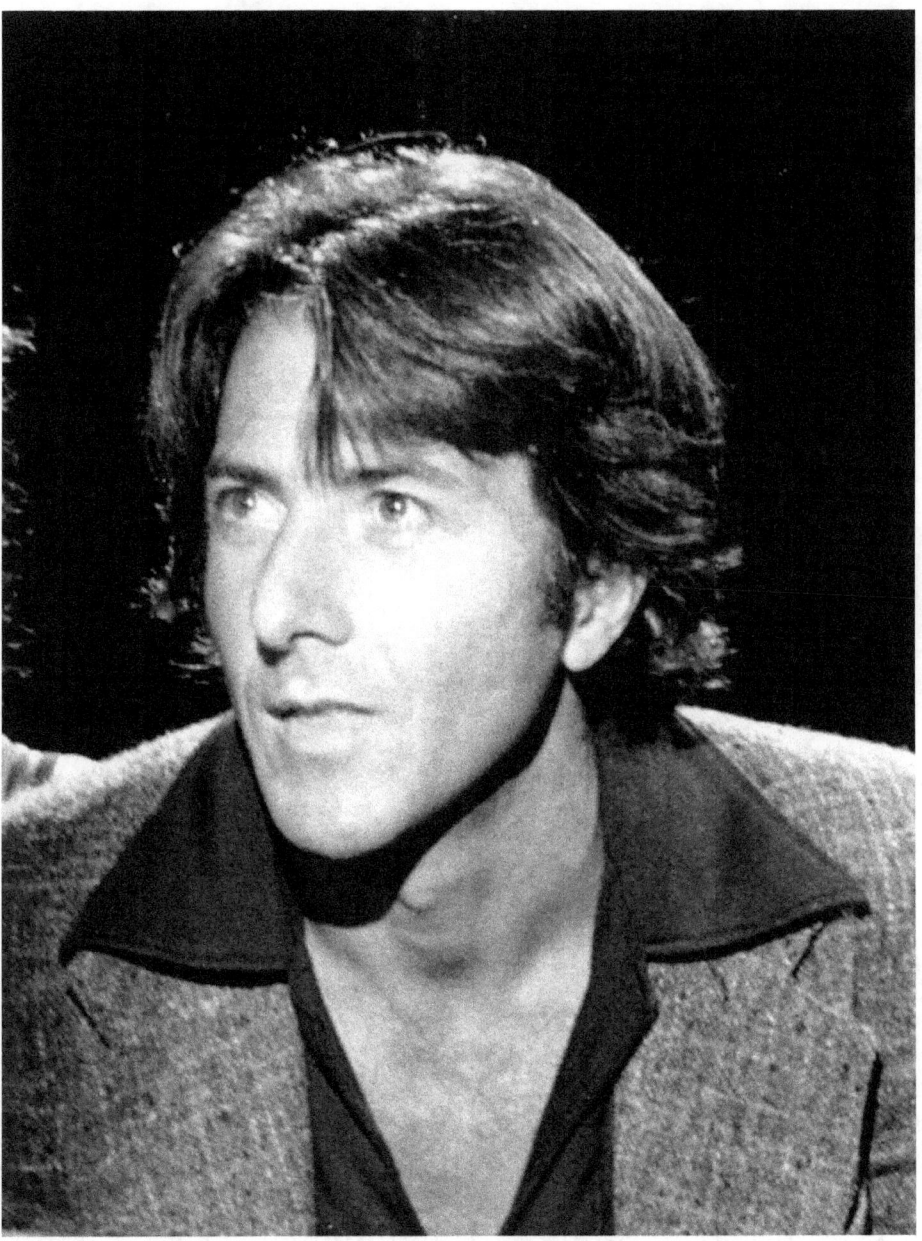

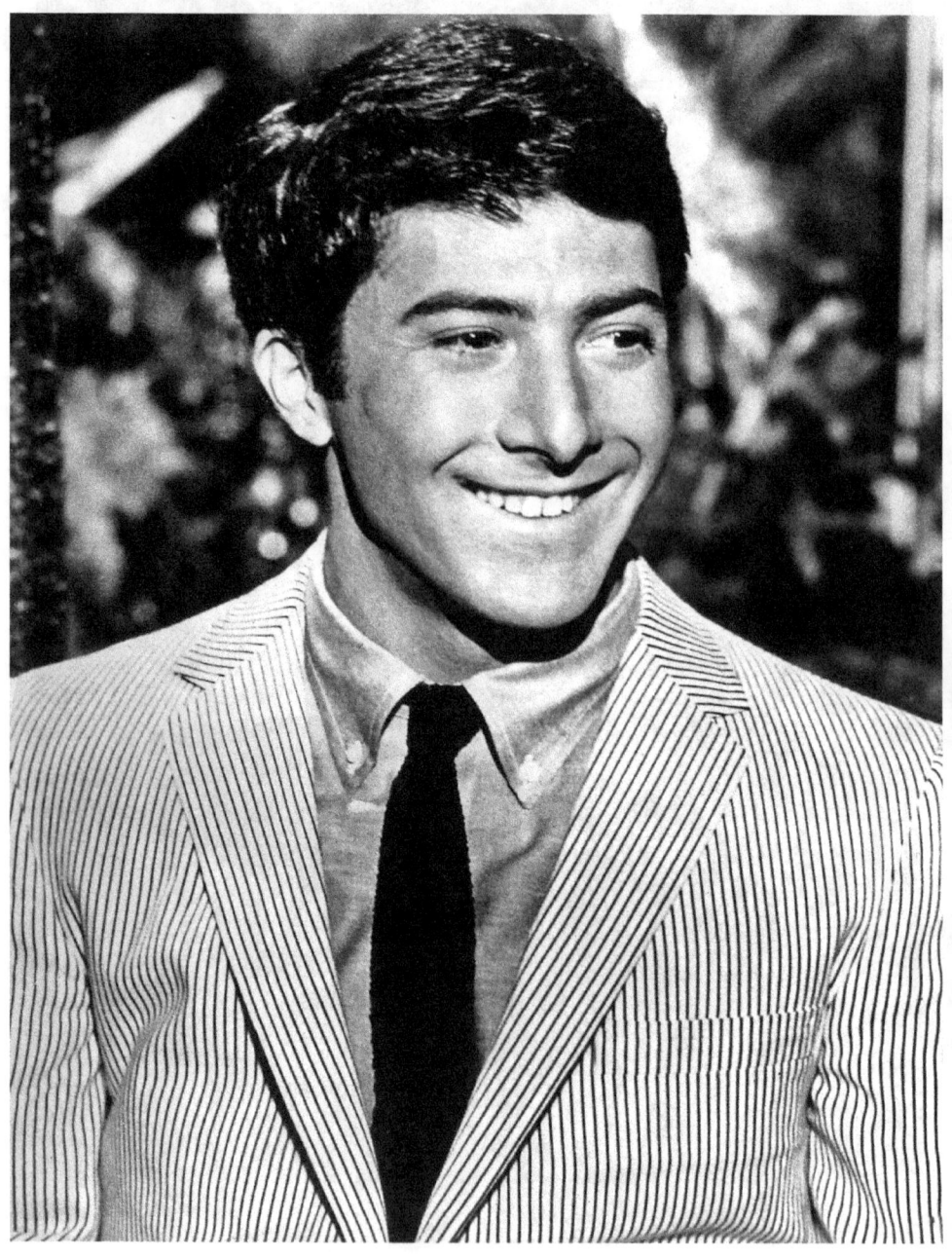

"Are You Here For An Affair?"

Benjamin Braddock, The Graduate and
Dustin Hoffman As Iconic Outsider

Few films in the history of cinema are true game changers. There are many that made instant stars of their leading actors, but the list is small when it comes to those that almost single-handedly altered the course of movie making. The Graduate is one of those rare movies, one that offered viewers something new, fresh and most importantly, a viewpoint they could understand. And the physical manifestation of the filmgoers shared angst was the unlikely Dustin Hoffman, a thirty year old actor who, to them at least, had appeared out of nowhere.

Many people believe that The Graduate was Dustin Hoffman's first movie role, but this is not the case. Yes it was his first starring role on the screen, but there had been minor parts in lesser movies filmed before it. His debut was in fact released in August of 1967, when he took a bit part in Arthur Hiller's otherwise now forgotten comedy, The Tiger Makes Out. It concerns Eli Wallach as Ben Harris, a New York postman who kidnaps a girl because he's run out of ideas of how to woo her. The problem is that he captures the wrong woman, not the one he'd been fancying, but a middle aged housewife with more "balls" than him, played nicely by Anne Jackson.

The Tiger Makes Out received some good notices back in the day, and though Hoffman had only a small role on the street as a character named Hap, critics were quick to point out the supporting cast, of which, of course, Hoffman was a member. Time Magazine wrote, quite accurately, "The near-perfect performances of Anne Jackson and Eli Wallach are augmented by a parade of outstanding character actors." Hoffman, who at this time had been playing on the stage to increasingly good notices for nearly a decade, had little to do in this fun but now rather dated romp, but the film did prove to be a valid experience for him.

There is one more film to "deal" with before we get to The Graduate, and that is Madigan's Millions, directed by Stanley Prager and filmed in 1966 before Hoffman's breakthrough but released after his unexpected success in 1967. Hopelessly cheesy today, this Italian-Spanish production is actually good fun. Easy to track down these days, it's mostly worth seeing for the chance to catch Dustin in such low brow and daft surroundings. He plays Jason Fister, a bespectacled agent looking for a million dollar debt owed by a dead mobster. Hoffman hams it up something rotten here, but his broad brush strokes fit suitably with the heavy handed material on offer. Madigan's Millions isn't exactly funny in the truest sense; it is however mostly enjoyable as an odd ball experience. Packaged and re-packaged over the years, usually to cash in on Hoffman's star status, it's harmless fun and though by no means a classic, it's a nice little curiosity for Hoffman fans.

If you are a newcomer to the cinematic world of Dustin Hoffman, there is no doubt that the first place you should go is The Graduate, the film that made him a star and showed the world, and indeed Dustin himself, just what he was capable of. If you have a passing interest in serious cinema then you've probably seen The Graduate before, but it's worth reiterating the importance of

Hoffman's performance within this very familiar and hugely iconic movie. It's the ultimate sixties role, epitomising the generation that came to age in that decade and how they were no longer willing to go along with the firmly-set rules of their elders. Without resorting to far out clichés, The Graduate becomes the great youth film of the sixties by casting not a cool, charismatic, traditionally good looking hipster in the lead role, but an awkward, out of place, disenchanted outsider. This is a young man whom everybody believes has a bright future; though ironically Benjamin himself doesn't know what he's going to do next, if indeed he feels like doing anything at all.

One of the key scenes arrives in the early part of the film, when Benjamin is reclining in the family pool, which features a vital quote: "Well it's very comfortable just to drift here," he tells his pushy, authoritative father, sunglasses shielding his eyes from the harsh rays of the sun, and the daunting glare of his own future.

When director Mike Nichols decided to adapt Charles' Webb's book to the screen, the production executives wanted a safe bet as far as casting the main protagonist was concerned. Benjamin Braddock was our eyes in this tale of a young man, fresh out of college, unexpectedly getting involved in an affair with the wife of his father's business partner. Mrs. Robinson, who is played wonderfully in the film by Anne Bancroft, has become the familiar ideal of the older woman syndrome, the ultimate face of the cougar, the mature lady bagging the younger man. Indeed, when it comes to myth and even vague knowledge of The Graduate, it is the iconic image of Hoffman's Braddock, framed under Mrs. Robinson's bare leg, which comes to mind. But The Graduate is about much more than an unlikely affair. The affair, of course, makes a "man" of Benjamin, and

Mrs Robinson's worldly experience brings him into adulthood on a literal level. The real worth of The Graduate however is not in the shallow affair; it's in the way Braddock attempts to adjust from teenage angst to manhood, even if the last thing he feels ready for is the onslaught of the adult world. The film's vital conflict, which sees Benjamin rebel from all authority, even Mrs Robinson, is brought about by his subsequent infatuation with the Robinson's young daughter, Elaine, played with straight forward class by Katharine Ross. All these elements combine to make The Graduate a perfect coming of age tale; but the star of the whole thing, and the man who embodies all the discomfort of this transformative shift into manhood, is Dustin Hoffman.

In the book, Braddock is a blonde haired, blue eyed young man, and the film studio wanted a typical leading man of the era to portray the part. Robert Redford was on the cards, but Nichols was adamant that the short, shuffling, uncomfortable and ill-fitting Hoffman had what it took to bring Braddock to life on the screen. The studio, understandably, thought him mad, but Nichols kept pushing, even if Hoffman himself was the last person who thought he was right for the role. His screen test, after all, had been a disaster, a love scene with Katharine Ross which Hoffman struggled through. He found it unbelievable for starters that Ross would be interested in someone like Hoffman. And Ross, for her part, agreed, saying Hoffman looked about three feet tall and seemed unkempt.

On the day of his audition, Hoffman dropped his subway tokens all over the floor. A crew member picked them up, handed them to Dustin and said, "Here kid, you're gonna need these." Despite the protests of everyone around him, Nichols cast Hoffman. Dustin was happy to land the part but also terrified, and found making the film a serious challenge. He never felt like he was delivering, and seeing the worried face of Mike Nichols behind the camera, was convinced the director had made a mistake. Exhausted one day and not delivering the goods for a vital scene, Nichols took him aside and said this film was going to be seen forever and ever, and if this scene didn't turn out right, Dustin would always remember it as the day he messed up. From then on, Dustin gave it his all and absorbed the lesson.

Nichols' gamble paid off, but casting Dustin was by no means a guarantee of success. Hoffman was very aware of this bold decision and was later shocked by the back lash. "As far as I'm concerned, Mike Nichols did a very courageous thing casting me in a part that I was not right for, meaning I was Jewish," Hoffman later said. "In fact, many of the reviews were very negative. It was kind of veiled anti-Semitism... I was called 'big-nosed' in the reviews... 'a nasal voice'."

He also recalled one review, which singled Hoffman out as a cretin, claiming he was terribly mis-cast. For Nichols, it was not his "Jewishness" which interested him, but the weird otherness he could bring to the role. Twitchy, nervous and uncomfortable in his own skin, Hoffman made Braddock that rare thing in the movies - a real person. We all feel like Braddock sometimes, especially as young men (or women), and Hoffman knew that feeling more than anyone.

As weird as Hoffman may have come across to traditional movie critics back in 1967, something about him appealed to young people. It was his awkwardness, his discomfort and his whole manner which made Braddock not only a believable figure in a film which could have easily descended into the ridiculous, but a figure ordinary people could relate to. Without Hoffman's involvement, The

Graduate could be forgotten today. Granted, it's wonderfully written, directed with stylish panache and brilliantly cast (Bancroft herself is perfect in the part), but it's Hoffman, unconventional and extremely likeable in his underwhelming presence, who makes The Graduate a classic. It may be a film of its time, but thanks to Hoffman's perfectly observed portrayal of a young man at a very important crossroads towards a self discovery he may not be finding any time soon, the film has outlived countless other films from the same era. It was a huge hit in its day, speaking directly to the generation gap of the late sixties. But today it looks as fresh as ever, and still feels relevant.

The film made Hoffman an instant celebrity, one of the biggest movie stars in the world and an icon to a whole generation. Still living in his modest New York apartment, Hoffman enjoyed his success and regularly invited fans, many of whom stayed permanently outside his building in hope of getting a glimpse of him, into his home for pleasant chats and refreshments. He was Dustin Hoffman, not Benjamin Braddock, but many admirers thought, and perhaps hoped, that he was. Like Bob Dylan, the youth of the sixties saw him as a kind of guru, someone who had the answers to the questions that were puzzling them. They soon learned of course that Hoffman was no prophet, just an actor looking to make a living and hopefully challenge himself along the way.

The key to Dustin's success as Braddock is in the little details. Firstly, it's that kooky "duck walk" as Pauline Kael called it, the jarring physicality which makes him stick out like a sore thumb, with both the grown ups and the students. His clumsy attempts to arouse Mrs Robinson are beautifully done too, especially in the scene where, blank faced and even bored himself, he places his hand on Mrs.

Robinson's breast, a gesture so stripped of passion that she barely even notices it and begins wiping a stain from the top she has just removed. There is also a lot of humour to be had in his voice, his vocal quirks, and those strange little murmurs he makes, especially when nervous in the bedroom, which were apparently lifted from Nichols himself.

"I looked at it as a character part," Hoffman said of Braddock, a character who happened to be almost a decade younger than him in reality. "I tried to remember what I felt like at that age back in 1958. I made no attempt to give it a feeling of the sixties. I've made a film that exploded but I am not responsible."

Hoffman's words, uttered not long after the release of the film, sum up what makes the performance so effective. Dustin said in 1969 that "when I get up and get into the bathroom, the Sound of Silence (Simon and Garfunkel's song, used in the movie) isn't playing," which is a lovely way to put it. It may have seemed like a perfectly natural portrayal of a young man at odds with his time, but Dustin had to work very hard to achieve that kind of world weariness that oozes from every pore of Benjamin Braddock. This, after all, was not Hoffman's generation, but he was able to channel his own earlier insecurities and bring them into Braddock, an unexpected icon for the age of free love. In reality he was a battle weary actor, someone who'd had so many doors slammed in his face he was probably confused why Nichols had opened this one for him.

"In those days," Hoffman told Time Out, "I hung out with Robert Duvall and Gene Hackman and we were certain we were never going to be romantic leads. I was waiting tables and Duvall was working all night at the post office. We just hoped to be character actors who could earn enough to make a living for the rest of our lives. When The Graduate came about, I didn't even want to try for it. I'd read the book and I thought it was a role made for Robert Redford. I was always going up for character juvenile roles – which meant you weren't attractive!'

"I was a freak accident," Hoffman later said of his success, "so I got a lead that happened to be The Graduate and it was like a light switch went on and I was an instant star. For most actors you start by playing euphemistically called supporting roles; it's not even the supporting role - it's less than that, and if you are lucky you build up to supporting roles and then to starring roles..."

It may have been out of the ordinary, but Hoffman's fame was no fad. For others, Dustin's emergence as a serious film performer broke down the gates. No longer did you have to look, sound and act a certain way in order for the masses to find you appealing. In fact, the standard now became old hat and the stars of the New Hollywood were just like you and me. For Hoffman, The Graduate was the first entry in a filmography full of towering moments and iconic performances. He did not follow it right up with another movie. Instead he went back to the New York theatre and thought hard about his next movie role. When he made the decision, it could not have been more different to The Graduate.

"What was the Baby Picture?"
Dustin Hoffman as Ratso Rizzo

If you take you average actor, the kind who's been yearning for big screen success for years, perhaps close to a decade, then the success of a film like The Graduate would understandably affect and boost the ego. The fame garnered by such a role might be infectious, giving you a certain power, but also facing you with a dilemma, as both an actor trying to keep his integrity, and more importantly, as a human being trying to hang on to who he is. Many actors would have fallen into the predictable trap, taken roles just like The Graduate's Benjamin Braddock in order to milk the fame for all it was worth, playing variations on the same character in order to stay in the headlines for another year or so, before fading back into obscurity, more than likely, uttering the words "It was good while it lasted..."

Of course, Hoffman being Hoffman, he did not go the predictable yet so tempting route. Dustin was offered boat loads of roles after the smash of The Graduate, but he found them too easy, safe and predictable; too Braddock-esque, and mere caricatures portraying the so called lost generation, at odds with their predecessors and looking for a truth of their own. Hoffman wanted to prove he was still the same character actor who'd tread the boards for minimum wage throughout the sixties, a man who took on each part as if it were an extra layer of skin, who lived the character and also wanted to challenge himself. When he accepted and agreed to play Rico "Ratso"

Rizzo in Midnight Cowboy, many people thought he was making the first big mistake of his professional career. This was it, they thought, he's blown it. He had started his filmography off with a perfect, appealing and quickly iconic role, redefining the rules of what a leading man could be and bringing in a wave of unconventional actors influenced by his awkward yet appealing performance. But here he was, taking an odd ball supporting role that most new stars wouldn't give the time of day.

Mike Nichols was one of the people who told Hoffman he was crazy. "I've given you this chance," he said, rather arrogantly, "and you're blowing it." As Hoffman later said though, the film might have made him a star, but it didn't make him an actor. Indeed, he'd been one of them for a decade, long before The Graduate.

Despite the warnings, Dustin took the second banana to Jon Voight's Midnight Cowboy, illustrating that fame had not gone to his head and he was in this for the work, wanting to be an equal member of the team contributing to a great work of art. And that is what Midnight Cowboy is, a truly great work of art.

"I was getting all these offers and they were all replicas," Dustin recalled. "I went back to the theatre for a bit. Then Midnight Cowboy came along and people tried to talk me out of doing that." Even if Nichols thought he was "undoing" the work he did on The Graduate to become a star, Hoffman was intent on playing Ratso and proving he was no one trick pony.

The plot concerns Joe Buck (a staggeringly good Voight), a naive Texan who heads to New York City to make it as a hustler, a "stud", and rake in the cash as a gigolo to rich New Yorkers. A few days in however, Joe realises New York isn't all he hoped it would be, and his hustling skills aren't quite up to snuff. He meets Ratso, a sleazy con man who hoodwinks Joe for twenty bucks and leaves him out to dry. Later, when Joe loses his apartment and runs out of cash, he begins to drift the streets, homeless, penniless and armed only with his portable radio, which he listens to throughout the film. When he bumps into Ratso again, the latter appears more pathetic, less a seedy hustler and more a sad figure of pity. Ratso convinces Joe to stay at his run down flat in a building which is due to be demolished. Though a crumbling, roach infested dump, it's better, and indeed warmer, than the streets. But Ratso has his sights on Florida, a healthy new life of sunshine and coconut milk, and when he begins to manage Joe's hustling activities, hopes to raise enough money for them both to flee the grimy streets of New York for fresh beginnings. As the two men get closer and their situation becomes more desperate, the dream of a new life together in Florida not only seems more appealing, but sadly, also less likely.

British director John Schlesinger had just come off the huge production of Far from the Madding Crowd and desired a smaller, more intimate project with less complications. Schlesinger certainly got that with Midnight Cowboy, and with his inventive direction gave the film its individual style. He looked at Midnight Cowboy with an outsider's eye, heightening our own sense of fear, dread and awe at this strange, vast city and the many assorted people who inhabit it. While Schlesinger presents us the many sides of New York from an unbiased if often slightly exotic perspective, Voight and Hoffman take us inside the kind of world we have seen in cities countless times, but only rush past rather than take in. They represent the drifters and outsiders existing on the fringes, the kind of people many avoid eye contact with. But in Midnight Cowboy we are plunged into that world, and convinced, quite easily in fact, into seeing them as human beings, complex souls with feelings and yearnings of their own.

The bond formed between Ratso and Joe, at the heart of the picture, is one of the most moving friendships in film history. It begins as a con for Ratso, a survivor cunningly aware that this wide eyed Southern gentleman will be easy to swindle. Joe's initial reaction when he encounters Ratso after the incident (Ratso sends Joe to O' Daniel, a supposed pimp who may be able to get him work, but actually turns out to be a religious nut) is pure rage. He roughs him up and demands his money back. Predictably, Ratso doesn't have it. After this the relationship takes an unexpected turn. When Ratso invites him to his hovel, in a fit of desperation, Joe is initially mistrustful. "You don't look like a fag," he says, wondering why this strange odd ball would think of holding out the hand of friendship. We soon learn however that Ratso is a tragic figure, hopelessly lonely and craving intimacy. Perhaps seeing that Joe is a kind hearted man, he reveals his softer side. Ratso makes him as comfortable as he can, settling him down on a bed and offering coffee, even removing his boots for him while he sleeps. He has been alone in these rough streets for a long time, but he finds his desired connection with Joe, who himself is searching for a relationship of meaning after a bad start in life (alluded to in flashbacks throughout the film). Even his hustling is a masked attempt to connect, to be seen, felt and touched. With Ratso, Joe finds the first deep and fulfilling relationship of his life. Many have raised the issue that there is a veiled homosexual subtext here, but I don't think it's as simple as that.

Homosexuality however, is a constant in the film, which seems appropriate, seeing as Schlesinger himself was a gay man just about to spread his wings and publicly embrace his sexuality. Schlesinger clearly inserted his own fears, insecurities and thoughts about homosexuality, and people's one dimensional perceptions of it, to come to conclusions of some kind with his characters and their predicaments. To use an example, Joe mostly makes his money from paid sex with gay men, most of whom are either repressed or full of shame, in acts which repulse Joe no end. But with Ratso there is a bond on a deeper level, and there's no question of it passing over into the physical. Sex for Joe Buck is a sleazy act, very separate from love and feelings, while primarily being the arena where he thinks he can prove his old fashioned manliness. Ironically, Buck actually struggles in these scenarios. Tellingly perhaps, during his sex with Brenda Vaccaro's character towards the end of the film, he fails to achieve an erection all together. Only when she mocks him, playfully that is, for his inability to rise to the occasion does he become over taken with passion, but it's done more to prove a point than being genuinely out of sexual arousal. The theory that Buck might be gay beneath his Southern machismo is at its most believable here, though it ultimately seems irrelevant to the core of the story.

More vital to Buck, and the whole film for that matter, is the importance of Ratso in his life. When they were making the movie, Hoffman told a journalist rather simplistically that Midnight Cowboy was about two men who love each other but do not engage in a homosexual relationship. Though they are unlikely chums to start with, Ratso's friendship gives him an intimacy that will stay with him long after the film is over and he begins his new life, albeit alone, in Florida.

But Ratso and Joe's relationship is not one dimensional, it's multi layered. At times Ratso comes across as a wife-like figure, even making meals for Joe and then dishing out the food out with the kind of fussiness often evident in a woman feeling unappreciated by her man. At other times, it's simply brotherly, but the kindness is from both sides. One of the most touching scenes comes before Joe and Ratso enter the freak out Warhol-esque party. Ratso, feeling ill, is sweating profusely on the staircase. With genuine gentle care, Joe takes his own shirt and wipes the sweat from Ratso's head, who clings on to Joe like a boy. In a heartbreaking moment, Ratso leans his head off his torso. The relationship has crossed a border; they are now more deeply bonded than it had seemed possible, thrust together in the mean streets of New York, firmly conjoined together against all odds.

Though one must credit Schlesinger's sensitive direction, Waldo Salt's fabulous screenplay and of course James Leo Herlihy for his original book, it's the strength of the acting, making these words and situations seem genuine and spontaneous, which elevates Midnight Cowboy into an immortal tale. Voight is so fresh and vital here that it's impossible to imagine anyone else in the role. During casting of the film, Hoffman did screen tests with Voight and other Joe Buck hopefuls. When asked who he thought was the best, Hoffman declined to use such a word to describe a fellow performer, but did admit that when he watched the screen tests back of the other actors, he was still watching himself in the scenes. When they rolled the Voight screen test, Hoffman could not keep his eyes off him. And that pretty much sums it up; Voight is contagiously watchable as Buck and one follows his tale with intense interest. He might easily have been a shallow, simple man who we did not care much for, but Voight lends him a sweetness, despite his often unsavoury acts, that ensures we genuinely care to the last frame and beyond.

Hoffman is spellbinding, not just for the obvious reasons, but for the way he shifts our pre-judgements into genuine feelings. Ratso is at first cinema's oiliest, grubbiest con man. Cleverly though, Dustin sheds several layers away to reveal the inner being, and he does it so subtly that we fail to pin point the moment when we began caring for rather than reviling him. The first moment we see there is more to this trickster is in the cafe scene when he removes his shoes to prove he has no change hidden in them, and we see his holey socks, revealing dirty toes. When he takes Buck back to his lair, it's gut wrenchingly sad the way he tries to make him at home, even pulling down the torn, dirty brown curtain to block out the light so Joe can get to sleep. It's in these little moments that Dustin makes Ratso a well rounded creation.

As Ratso becomes more ill, Hoffman the man disappears and only Ratso remains. It's a complete tour de force, from the thick accent and the dodgy mannerisms to the painful cough and quirky limp. Ratso could have easily turned out a mere cartoon, a broad caricature, but Hoffman makes him a human, a sympathetic character we not only grow fond of, but start to genuinely like and understand. When Ratso talks about his childhood and his late father, a shoe shiner whose hands were so dirty he had to be buried with gloves on, we are utterly heartbroken, yet we also grasp that Ratso's fate was forever set in stone. The finale, as heart breaking as it is, is inevitable. In order for Joe Buck the cowboy hustler to fade into the past as the new Joe Buck arrives, fresh faced and positive, Ratso has to die; indeed, with his death is a rebirth.

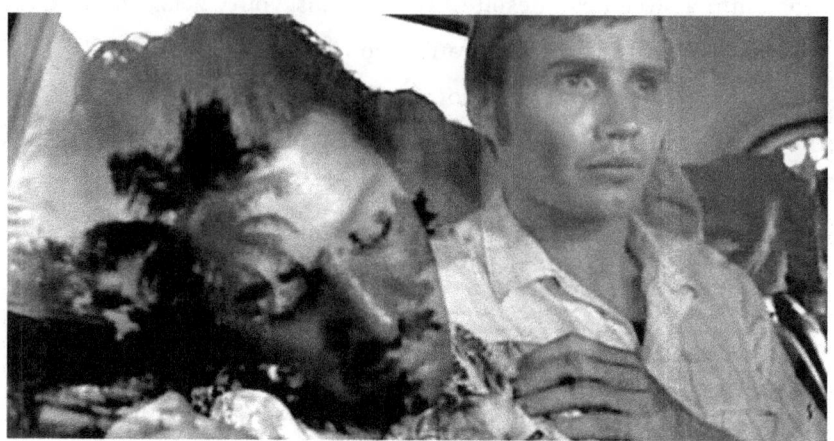

The final shot of Midnight Cowboy, with a protective Joe Buck holding on to his fallen comrade, Rico "Ratso" Rizzo.

Hoffman once said an interesting thing in an interview with Charlie Rose. He said that when walking in the street he often gazes at a homeless person or a derelict and wonders "What's the baby picture?" He wonders what happened to make them that way, what changed in their lives to derail them so harshly? Hoffman was clearly thinking the same thing when he played Ratso. Looking at the part as if he was a real man, Dustin could construct a past for him. Why was he on the streets? What happened in *his* life to make him forever known as Ratso? What could Rico have been?

I believe Midnight Cowboy is not only one of the five best films of Hoffman's career, but one of the finest movies of the past fifty years. It won Best Picture at the Oscars, the first X rated film to do so, and I have to say no film has deserved the plaudit more than this. It made a huge sum at the box office; unexpectedly, given the subject matter and also considering the people behind this film made it for the art, not commercial gain. Today, of course, it's a sad fact that Midnight Cowboy would be put out in a few art house theatres and quickly disappear out of sight.

Notices were strong, but not all reviews were glowing. Some saw the film as a mere series of set ups, with Hoffman and Voight shining despite what they saw as the flaws. Roger Ebert for one was not totally bowled over, though I do believe he got it wrong for once. "Midnight Cowboy comes heartbreakingly close to being the movie we want it to be," he wrote, adding, "The performances have a flat, painful accuracy. The world of Times Square, a world of people without hope and esteem, seems terribly real. Here is America's underbelly and it even smells that way. And seeing these things and reaching to them, we are ready to praise the movie where we found them. And cannot. There has been a failure somewhere in the director's faith in his materials. John Schlesinger has not been brave enough to tell his story and draw his characters with the simplicity they require. He has taken these magnificent performances, and his own careful perception of American society, and dropped them into an offensively trendy, gimmick-ridden, tarted-up, vulgar exercise in fashionable cinema. Trying to get the good out of Midnight Cowboy is like looking at a great painting through six inches of Jell-O. It is there -- the greatness is there -- but unworthy hands have meddled with it almost beyond repair."

Many critics hailed it however, and everybody agreed that the acting was superb. Hoffman earned Oscar and Golden Globe nominations, plus critical acclaim. He proved, as one reviewer observed, that he was no Mike Nichols invention. Hoffman, at this stage, was capable of anything, and his Ratso is a real showcase, a transformative role that may have been influenced by his own theatrical performances, but quickly overtook any comparisons to his past, or anyone else's for that matter, and became a truly original piece of work. There never was, and has never been again, a performance quite like it.

Though some of the themes may be old fashioned now (the Warhol party is so swinging it's virtually stuck in that era, and views towards homosexuality have thankfully moved on since) the central friendship between Joe and Ratso, two outsiders against the world, fighting for their place, is as moving and powerful as ever.

"I Have A Horse... and Four Wives."

Dustin Hoffman in Little Big Man

The same year Dustin Hoffman emerged as cinema's brightest star of the New Hollywood wave, director Arthur Penn had caused waves of outrage across the globe with his bloody, violent and perversely appealing on screen portrayal of Bonnie and Clyde, the seminal biopic which starred Warren Beatty and Faye Dunaway as the doomed crooks and helped change the tide of filmmaking in the late 1960s. Following 1969's Alice's Restaurant, Penn eyed up his next film, this one a slyly comic epic western based on Thomas Berger's novel, Little Big Man.

If Bonnie and Clyde had made us see the human side of violent criminals, Little Big Man forced modern audiences to take a look in the mirror and accept that Native Americans were not the bad guys Hollywood always made them out to be. Little Big Man, though far fetched at points, has a good heart, a conscience and something new to say. In an era when the accepted norm was being challenged, and the biased history books being reassessed, Little Big Man stands high as a laudable product of its time, a film which encouraged the world to reassess their warped views on American colonialism.

The only man Penn could picture as the star was Dustin Hoffman, modern film's great shape shifting method actor. Hoffman plays Jack Crabb, a 121 year old man speaking to a dubious and rather cynical historian in a hospice in 1970. He begins to recall his life story and the many outrageous adventures he has been through; though whether one chooses to believe him or not is another matter. Crabb claims to have been a child survivor of a massacre and taken in by Indians, where he was given the nickname "Little Big Man" for his shortness and bravery. As his tale goes on, Crabb is caught by the US cavalry as a teenager and denies any involvement with the Indians in order to survive. He then becomes a fraudulent snake oil merchant, and when reunited with his long lost sister becomes a gunslinger by the name of the Soda Pop Kid, where he encounters the mythical Wild Bill Hickok. He moves on to working in a shop, gets married and is double crossed by his partner, causing Jack to relocate. Later on, Jack meets up with his childhood friend, Younger Bear, while seeking his wife who was abducted during a siege. He then begins working for General Custer, by accident as it happens, and takes part in an attack against the Indians. His adventures go on, as he flips back and forth with forced loyalty, at one point living as a bearded hermit, before working with Custer again and tricking the power mad General into an ambush at the Battle of Little Bighorn. Near the end, he shares a symbolic moment on a hill top with the ageing Indian Old Lodge Skins, which stands as one of the film's most important sequences, as well as its funniest.

Though highly comedic in parts, Little Big Man is tinged with tragedy. There is a heavy sadness in Crabb's recollections, that he misses that old world, the brave Indian people, and feels ashamed to be of the kind who eradicated those honest and pure natives. History has got it all wrong, but nothing Crabb says will rebalance the injustice and the negative light in which the world still chooses to paint the Native Americans. As he closes his story and tells the historian to leave, all the comedic light of Little Big Man turns to sorrowful blackness and heavy shame. Crabb, like mankind, cannot reverse time.

Though the film is honourable as it stands firmly on the side of the Indians, there are numerous historical inaccuracies, though thankfully they do not ruin the enjoyment of the film, nor the power behind its defiant message. The man who bore the name Little Big Man was a genuine Native American leader, though his story has no similarity to Crabb's. Minor inaccuracies, such as Wild Bill Hickok's death, are irrelevant, especially when considering that it's our personal choice whether to believe Crabb's recollections or not. Some American purists may have been offended by the depiction of Custer as a raving mad man, but the filmmakers did not intend for realism on Custer's portrayal; in fact, they were poking fun at him, and through a satirical slant were able to make such an over the top depiction seem perfectly acceptable. And though some historians might argue whether Custer was as cruel as he's made out to be, and in fact harboured sympathy for the Indians and their plight, his lunacy gives Crabb's recollections a relatable simplicity they would have lacked if following actual historical events step by step.

What is certain though, and not up for debate, is the fact that Crabb's character is loosely based on a man named Curley, a Native American scout who worked for Custer. Fittingly, Curley himself has been doubted by historians. In interviews the older Curley claimed to be the last survivor to witness or be involved in Custer's Last Stand, though the truth of his involvement in the battle has so many yarns spun around it that it seems impossible to come to an acceptable version of the truth. Either way, Curley has a lot in common with the boastful, though good hearted Jack Crabb.

Seeing as though he is in nearly every scene and remains the central character throughout, this is every bit Hoffman's show from beginning to end, and he delivers a staggering performance. Totally believable as the aged Crabb in heavy make up, we forget we are watching Dustin and not a craggy, bedraggled survivor from the Wild West. The legendary Dick Smith applied the make up, bringing his usual authenticity to the role, which also aided Dustin in his portrayal of old age. Hoffman told Life Magazine there was no way you couldn't feel like an old man wearing this heavy latex. To get the right effect for the old man's voice, Hoffman would sit in his dressing room and scream for an hour to tire out his vocal cords.

Seeing as Dustin's character goes from his teenage years to extreme old age, it's a credit to his abilities that every age he portrays, and every scene he plays, is utterly convincing. While most of the film is tinged with a comedic edge, and avoids melodrama even when dealing with the more tragic moments, it comes across as a wonderfully observed and perfectly executed tour de force. This was his third showcase performance, after The Graduate and Midnight Cowboy, and was just as effective as the now more iconic and legendary roles that came before it. There's a naturalness here, or at least the illusion of naturalness, that makes you believe Crabb's every word, whether telling it or acting it out. One gets the sense that he means it, even if it isn't all totally true, which of course makes it true to him and us the viewer. Hoffman's straight forward portrayal of Crabb carries us through the ludicrous ups and downs, and had a lesser actor taken the part, Little Big Man could have turned out a lot different. In short, it could have been a total misfire. But Hoffman pulls it off, proving again that in the sixties and seventies he had few if any true equals as a screen actor.

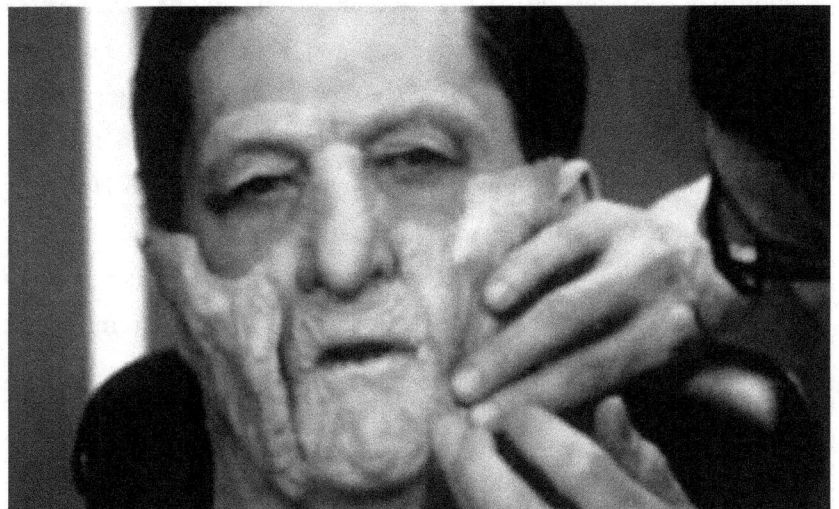

Hoffman, completely unrecognisable, during make up before a day's shooting on Little Big Man.

In an on-set interview, a tired looking Hoffman spoke of the role. "How do you prepare for a role, the mechanical things you do, the psychological things, how do you do a guy from 15 to 121?" he pondered. "It's difficult to answer because the question is like the one put forth to a painter or a sculptor, but not a movie actor. You don't have time. Most of the time there's no rehearsal. I'd talk a bit with the director, read the script and then get to work. I couldn't ride a horse so I had to learn... The character sweeps all over the place, he lives with the whites, he lives with the Indians. There are many faces, though he's the same character; he was young, in his twenties, his thirties, he had a beard, a moustache, he had an aged face. One thing that's an actor's job is to know as much about himself as he can. The more things he knows the more he can use of himself."

Hoffman also related to the fact that Crabb didn't quite know where his world was, or where he belonged. He also raised concerns that in such a violent world, where we are surrounded by horror and war, he felt like a weak person "going from movie to movie while horrible things are happening." And it's clear that in Crabb Hoffman saw every side of his own personality, and was struck that it made him think about his own views on violence, both his pacifism and his more primitive urge to react, and put them all into the remarkably multi layered role.

"You do know there are certain things about a character," he added, "that you bring from yourself." No truly great film character is black and white and even the most villainous have positive or even likeable traits. Crabb is all man and every man; a coward, a hero, a weakling, a fighter, a family man, a loner, someone who belongs and then doesn't belong; he is loyal and yet often cowardly, a man to stand up and a man to run. Beneath the often wildly comic shenanigans in Little Big Man is a character we can all relate to. We don't have to be a hero all of the time, because often life is about surviving. Hoffman makes this clear as Crabb, an extremely likeable and far from perfect man in a gruesome, ruthless landscape. He may have been thinking of his own views on the Vietnam War and Penn clearly alludes to the brutality and cruelty of that particular conflict, but Little Big Man transcends the era in which it was made and remains a seminal, important piece of work. It can be about any time, yesterday, today or a hundred more years from now.

Little Big Man was another box office hit for Hoffman's expanding career and he received much acclaim for his work, including a BAFTA nomination. Reviews were highly positive, with Roger Ebert more convinced with this one than previous Hoffman films. Giving it 4 stars, he wrote "Arthur Penn's Little Big Man is an endlessly entertaining attempt to spin an epic in the form of a yarn."

Retrospectively, it tends to garner a lot of praise. Rather than being seen as merely a historical film, one released at a time when attitudes towards the true darkness of modern American's foundation were controversial, it's often picked out as a seventies highlight for storytelling and sheer entertainment alone. "The film's attitudes toward indigenous people were boldly progressive at the time of its release," wrote Jason Bailey for New York Times, "coming as it did during a period when most Westerns still teemed with racist images of 'merciless Indian savages'. But Little Big Man is more than a corrective; Hoffman's masterly acting, Penn's energetic direction and the sly wit of Calder Willingham's screenplay make for an unpredictable and inspired ride."

Other reviewers today seem to think it jars, never sitting comfortably between comedy and serious drama. Empire, in their modern reviews, give it a non-committal three stars, while Pop Matters criticised it for various reasons, writing, "For all the material's gravity, an absurdist spirit leavens the proceedings. Beguilingly shambolic and relentlessly anarchic, the movie is filled with anecdotal incidents, as befitting a possessed raconteur's yarn. Not all of it works. The old-school slapstick and rim-shot punchlines have a whiff of condescension, aside from being less funny than they should be. Hoffman, playing against type, doesn't help either. He may be right for the part physically, but he lacks the spontaneity and adroitness of the great physical comedians. (There's too much thinking in that feathered head.) All the mugging and anachronisms prove alienating, no doubt deliberate on Penn's part. His Brechtian approach seeks to distance the audience and invite contemplation at the same time."

It is of course, in my view at least, this kind of "Brechtian approach" which made many epic tales of self discovery from this period work so well. One cannot help but draw comparisons with Lindsay Anderson's surreal adventure, O Lucky Man (1973), a different film in many ways, but Brechtian in its style, and similar in its scope, sense of humour and heightened realism. But Little Big Man could also be seen as a pre-cursor to the more well known Forest Gump, in which a man recalls a remarkable life that seems too far fetched to be true, putting him in the centre of several major historical events. Unlike Gump however, Jack Crabb is smart enough to have a conscious about the world he exists in, and be all too aware of the damage done in the name of so called progress. Thanks to Hoffman's sensitive performance, Little Big Man remains to this day, almost fifty years on, a remarkable film with a big heart. It is also Hoffman's most complete performance, where he takes on every age of man and shines a mirror back at the audience. He'd never land such a part again, though he would develop as an artist in other, perhaps even more challenging ways.

The "Right" Choice

The Overlooked Films of Dustin Hoffman
in the 1970s

When discussing Dustin Hoffman's career in the 1970s, there are a number of films one would immediately jump to. Kramer vs. Kramer, the role which earned him an Oscar, seems like the most likely, while many would also pick out Marathon Man, Straw Dogs and Lenny as highlights. There are a number of movies in this time however, that were deemed odd ball choices. Some of these pictures quickly faded into time, though many are worth dusting off and re-assessing. I will explore them in the following article.

One of the now lesser known films from Hoffman's golden period is the curious Who is Harry Kellerman and Why Is He Saying Those Terrible Things About Me, in which he plays rock composer Georgie Soloway, looking for the man of the title who's been spreading lies about him. (To not spoil it for first time viewers, Kellerman's true identity is very surprising.) The film follows Soloway's life in the passing of one day, delving into his psychological troubles, his tormented past and his weirdest fantasies.

When I was collecting Hoffman films as a teenager in the pre-internet days, this title was a mystery to me; not only for its long title, but also due to Hoffman's appearance in the movie, judging from stills in film books. Dustin was attracted to the part because it was a deep character he could really get to grips with, and as it was a small, lowish budget film, he was destined to be at the very centre of it. It was also a drastically different character to what viewers had seen him play before, at least on the screen. Only four years earlier he'd embodied post-teen, pre-adulthood frustration in The Graduate, and played the ultimate outsider in Midnight Cowboy. And here he was, playing an even more complex part, a man who wrote love songs for a living but had never had a meaningful relationship of his own.

It may have been a good opportunity for Hoffman the actor (it was rather like one of the stage roles he'd played in the mid sixties), yet commercially speaking it was suicide after the smash hits that came before it. But Hoffman was not commercially minded, thankfully, and he took roles for their artistic worth, not the pay cheque attached to them.

Unfortunately, the film itself didn't match the work Hoffman put into it. Ulu Grosbard, who would work with Dustin again at the end of the 1970s, directs this free flowing, experimental and often daring film with just the kind of showiness it needs, but there is something slightly off about the whole thing. As good as Hoffman is in a difficult role in the middle of an awkward film, it doesn't always add up. That said, the savage critical mauling it received at the time was hardly valid, for it's certainly an entertaining and ambitious effort that deserves applauding for what it aims at more than damning for what it is.

For Hoffman, it was a worthwhile experience. As in earlier and later films, the role proved helpful to his personal life and own psychology. Soloway, like Hoffman at the time, knew all too well that success did not automatically bring happiness. "I used to think that if I became successful everything would fall into place. But that's not how it is. I have to tell you I don't feel different at all," Dustin said at the time. He may have been talking about himself, but the line could also have been plucked from this film. The personal attachment to the part is what makes this performance something special, better in fact than the film which often struggles to contain it. Though it was panned, Hoffman still got glowing mentions, and anyone seriously interested in his work, or unconvinced of his range back in the sixties and seventies, will be in awe. It really is worth your time.

One of the downright weirdest films of Hoffman's early period is Alfredo, Alfredo, released in 1973, a now forgotten Italian comedy which cast him as a mild mannered bank worker who struggles through a marriage to a domineering woman (played by Stefania Sandrelli) and toys with the idea of divorce (which is illegal) when planning to leave her for another woman, played by Carla Gravina.

Working for director Pietro Germi would have been an exciting opportunity for an actor like Hoffman, an American actor very much in tune with the European sensibility. Not only was he a master of comedy (Divorce Italian Style remains a classic), he was also the kind of director who might have been open to Hoffman's way of working. Hoffman, though a huge star at the time, was not one to let ego get in the way of a promising part, and he took the film on without hesitation.

Though Germi had already covered these themes on past pictures, there is a freshness to Alfredo, Alfredo that warrants its existence. It's energetically directed and performed, while Germi's script (a collaboration with three other screenwriters) is sharp and imaginative. The main ingredient which elevates the movie however is Hoffman's hilarious and well observed performance. While lesser stars would have gone for predictable safe choices and gone on auto pilot for the fat pay slips, Hoffman was keen to take risks and explore new avenues. His Alfredo is one of the quirkiest from his gallery of characters, and while it's never picked out as a highlight, it's a role which illustrates his range, not to mention his comic ability, so rarely mentioned in reference to Hoffman. But Alfredo is not that drastic a leap for Hoffman, for if one looks closer, even his most iconic roles have a lot of humour in them; Midnight Cowboy's Ratso would be a comic tour de force if not for the hints of tragedy, while no one could say Benjamin Braddock wasn't a comic character. Here, in the context of European satire, Hoffman amazingly doesn't seem out of place.

Again, it's indicative of his seemingly endless abilities in that golden period that the performance works, even if his efforts did garner criticism from some reviewers. "Passive as a potato," the New York Times wrote, "timid as a fawn, Dustin Hoffman is cast as a victim once again in Alfredo, Alfredo. Here, he has almost returned to his role in The Graduate: the innocent manchild overwhelmed by a devouring woman. The problem is that Dustin Hoffman isn't Italian. Despite his efforts to tear into his food with a Latin gusto, or the slicked-down hair above the urban American face, he simply can't appear to be a native of a provincial Italian town. However, there are beguiling details throughout. Mr. Hoffman's small, cautious smiles, the way his mouth and nostrils quiver when he smells his detested wife's perfume, and her scalp-chilling screams at the moment of orgasm—which alarm the neighbours and terrify the dog into fits of barking—all make for moments of fine farce."

Indeed, it is a performance full of subtleties that enhance this curious but appealing performance, in a film which may have aged but remains an entertaining little social satire.

Perhaps the most mainstream and commercial film Hoffman appeared in during the seventies, and therefore in my view the oddest of all, was Papillon (1973), an epic prison escape movie which paired him up with, however unlikely it may have seemed, Steve McQueen, the most macho and popular action screen star of the period. The film, based on Henri Charriere's autobiographical novel of the same name, follows McQueen as Charriere, unlawfully convicted of a murder and sent to a French prison for life. There he meets the intelligent embezzler and master cheat Louis Dega, played by Hoffman, who offers to help Charriere be freed. The pair become friends, suffering torturous life in a labour camp before Charriere is placed in solitary confinement after a botched escape plan. The film follows his struggles to become a free man in an unfair, cruel system.

Shot in Spain and Jamaica, the film had a then huge budget of 12 million dollars, by far the biggest film Dustin had been a part of up to that point. Henri Charriere acted as the film's on set consultant, perhaps explaining its gritty believability. Having the real subject of the film there at all times no doubt helped director Franklin J Schaffner, who was able to capture the kind of authenticity that would be sorely lacking in more schlocky prison break movies. Indeed, by the end of this arguably over long adventure film, one feels so exhausted and abused it's as if we too have been inside Devil's Island with McQueen and Hoffman.

Oddly, considering one lead was an unashamed star and the other a character actor, Hoffman and McQueen make a good on screen duo.

McQueen does his usual thing of being calm and collected, but it's Dustin who delivers the truly captivating performance. Again he disappears into the role, completely unrecognizable from the Hoffman we saw on his recently released picture, the academic gone feral in Straw Dogs. Here he plays the sneaky, bespectacled crook, as unappealing and drab as McQueen is cool and iconic. Hoffman's knack has always been the theatrical character role, the eccentric caricature he transforms into a multi layered puzzle, and here he is remarkably good in a challenging part. It's not so much the film itself that's underrated; it's Hoffman's performance within it.

Papillon was promoted as Hollywood's return to the "big movie" format of the golden period. Hoffman, to his credit, was not opposed to appearing in a mainstream film, just as his stardom did not prevent him from appearing in smaller art films, even foreign features. Contrary to some reviewers, he does well in these mainstream surroundings, which may well be a jazzed up prison escape B movie, but is also a good romp that also feels painfully real, brutally frank and evocative of true purgatory.

Papillon was a massive box office hit, though critics thought it to be so-so, if not a miss altogether. Roger Ebert opened his review by calling it "an expensive, exhaustive, 150-minute odyssey that doesn't so much conclude as cross the finish line and collapse. It has been outfitted with expensive stars and a glossy production, but it doesn't really make us care. When Steve McQueen finally escapes from Devil's Island we're happy more for ourselves than for him: Finally we can leave, too. Hoffman is using his limp again from Midnight Cowboy, and McQueen squints into the sun a lot, and that's about it."

One of Hoffman's most underrated pictures from his golden era is Straight Time, released in 1978, a quirky crime drama/thriller that was actually a minor box office hit at the time, and received a wave of positive reviews, but has become a little buried in time. For Hoffman, it was a real challenge to play a seedy outsider not designed to raise any sympathy from the viewer. Like all of Hoffman's best performances, his characters exist as whom they are whether we like it or not. We rarely, if ever, are led or manipulated into feeling anything for them, other than what we choose to.

Max Dembo, the part he plays in Ulu Grosbard's Straight Time, a film adapted from Eddie Bunker's book, No Beast So Fierce, is a sleazy small time crook, just out of prison and trying to adjust to life back on the outside. M Emmet Walsh delivers a brilliant performance as his patronising parole officer, attempting to get Max on the work ladder and back on the straight and narrow. Inevitably though, Max struggles with life as a clean living, law abiding citizen. He meets Jenny (played by Theresa Russell), who works at the employment agency, and agrees to go on a date with him, after which they strike up a romantic relationship. Despite such positive influences, it isn't long before Max is back in trouble, when his parole officer finds evidence of drug abuse in his room, paraphernalia actually left there by his friend (Gary Busey). Max ends up temporarily incarcerated, and angrier than ever with a system that continuously fails him, finds himself dragged back into crime. He takes part in a bank robbery with his old friend, Jerry, played by the late and brilliant Harry Dean Stanton, which proves fatal for his aims at a clean life.

The good thing about Straight Time is how low key it is, though not for one minute am I suggesting it's in any way flat. It's very realistic in fact, with no unnecessary dramatic fireworks flying around, and completely lacking in sentimentality. Not once is it suggested that we should get our violins out for Max and shake our fists at the unfairness of post-prison life, the inevitability of being pulled back in. We neither like nor dislike Dembo, but accept who he is and who he will always be. It makes it easier not to be swept either way because Hoffman's portrayal of him is so utterly flawless. He has all the hallmarks of the con who can't shake off the dishonest way of thinking; the twitchy physical mannerisms, the controlled voice and the detached emotional distance give us the feeling he could walk away from anyone or anything just in order to survive. It was another critical smash for Hoffman, with Gene Siskel noting that "Credit ultimately must go to Hoffman, who continues to avoid playing the million-dollar cardboard roles that so many of his peers are drawn to." The LA Times agreed that Dustin had delivered another tour de force, commenting, "Hoffman's Max has less dimension than some of his earlier characterizations. You wish his fight to go straight had gone on a little longer. But his cool, hard disillusion, his unsentimental realism and his fatalistic attitude toward a life that never got going makes its own impact."

As it happens, Hoffman was actually down to direct the film in its early stages, but he handed the job to the more experienced Grosbard when his insecurities got the better of him. Despite the added legal complications surrounding the film, specifically between Hoffman and the company First Artists, Straight Time came out well; and though it did not set the world alight, over the years it's acquired a cult status.

To his credit, Dustin Hoffman continued to choose roles he found interesting and engaging, regardless of their size, scope or potential commercial appeal. In 1976 he turned down an offer from Steven Speilberg to take the lead role in Close Encounters of the Third Kind. Hoffman said it was the best script he'd ever read but passed, for varying reasons. Hoffman recently admitted he was frightened that it would be such a huge hit that he would get attention on a whole other level. He also added that he would feel guilty and unworthy to be part of such a success. Either way, he's gone down as the man to turn down as many classics as he's starred in, often for such reasons.

Instead he took the lead in a smaller film, filmed in the UK, directed by Michael Apted, and based on the mysterious 11 days that mystery writer Agatha Christie disappeared. The film project began when Kathleen Tynan was investigating Christie's story for a BBC documentary and she informed producer David Puttman that it would make an in intriguing film.

In the picture, Vanessa Redgrave plays Christie, who after a car crash flees the scene and heads off to Harrogate in Yorkshire, booking herself into the Old Swan Hotel. Leaving a fake suicide note in the car, she is temporarily living by the fake name of Theresa Neele. Dustin Hoffman plays Wally Stanton, an American reporter intrigued by the whole affair and eager to get to the bottom of it.

Wonderfully shot by Apted, the film has a class and grace to it which makes it a treat for the eyes. The script is smooth and the locations (only a few miles from where I live) look beautiful. The performances are splendid, with Redgrave as brilliant as ever, bringing both strength and vulnerability to her role. Hoffman is wonderful too in one of his subtlest and most precise efforts of the

1970s. It's odd to think his part was originally intended for a tall blonde Englishman, a re-casting contrast reminiscent of The Graduate. It was in fact written as a supporting role, and was only fleshed out when Hoffman signed up.

For such a seamless looking picture, it's a surprise to learn the production was a stressful one for Dustin, who had just come off the filming of Straight Time. While the writers were in the middle of revisions on the script, the cameras were already ready to roll. Rightfully worried, Hoffman begged them to delay filming for two weeks, but they refused and the shoot went on as planned. During their break, after weeks of filming through the day and rewriting at night, the cast and crew relaxed while Dustin went off to help with the editing of Straight Time, before jetting back to quickly complete his scenes for Agatha. Such trivia aside, Agatha does not feel like a film that was wrought with production problems. It's an enjoyable and imaginative fantasy about what may or may not have happened to Agatha Christie in that lost period. Almost forgotten today, it remains a worthwhile viewing for fans of Hoffman.

Many fans of Hoffman's work will no doubt be aware of the movies mentioned in this piece, but those who aren't will hopefully want to seek them out. Not all of them are easy to get a hold of, but they are all worthy of your intensive detective work.

"I Don't Know My Way Home..."

Hoffman Becomes A Peckinpah Man in Straw Dogs

Many of Dustin Hoffman's films, including Midnight Cowboy and Little Big Man, had been controversial in their own way; but none of them compared to the outrage and shock spread by Straw Dogs. Directed by Hollywood outlaw Sam Peckinpah, the very man who had already made what was in his and many other's minds the ultimate statement on violence, 1968's The Wild Bunch, Straw Dogs opened up a whole new can of worms and raised issues which were not only uncomfortable for most film viewers, but utterly repellent. The film was a violation of everything about modern life, society and relationships we held with assurance. It didn't so much as break down barriers, but pulverise them into debris.

Based on Gordon M Williams' novel The Siege of Trencher's Farm, it was transformed by screenwriter David Zelag Goodman and Peckinpah into a moralistic and ultimately twisted modern western, a tale of territorial machismo in which violence proved, once and for all in Pechinpah land at least, to be the only proof of masculinity.

American mathematician David Sumner (Hoffman) and his wife Amy (Susan George) relocate to the Cornish village where she grew up, in search for some peace and quiet while he works on his latest book project. Instead of being a haven however, the remote dwelling turns out to be a war zone of worries, when the workmen doing repairs on the depilated roof, one of whom is a former boyfriend of

Amy's, begin to make life difficult for him. The film slowly descends into a three way face off between the gang, David and his discontented wife.

In theory Straw Dogs could have been a straight forward good-versus-bad tale of a man defending his honour and wife against evil. But this being Peckinpah, it is anything but as straight forward as that. Though the menacing brutes who always seem to be hanging around appear to be the true threat in the film, the real damaging tension is triggered by David and Amy's strained, if not crumbling marriage. He refuses to be the man she wants him to be, providing neither the emotional or sexual satisfaction she craves. While her sexuality and physicality can reduce the workmen to dribbling idiots, it also inadvertently invites unwanted (or subconsciously wanted, depending on how you look at it) sexual desire. When Amy shows a bare leg to the workers, or stands topless by the window while they are working on the roof, it's like a red rag to a bull. Still, the consequences of her openly flirtatious behaviour are way beyond, and much viler, than anything she could have foreseen.

The film is most famous, or perhaps infamous, for its graphic rape sequence, which has been misinterpreted over the years and taken out of context. Modern understanding is that Amy is enjoying the forced sex; that yes means no, not just for Amy, but for any woman. Though I am careful not to defend Peckinpah's chauvinism, there is much more to the scene than that. The set up for the scenario is vital; the men have tricked David into sitting and waiting in the middle of a field, under the pretence that they are hunting ducks, while Charlie, the workman who once had a brief fling with Amy, heads off to the house to see her. The initial sex between Charlie begins as a rape, where he slaps and threatens more extreme violence if she relents; but then he begins to show some tenderness, and it seems she has some strange, twisted affection for him. Amy is so starved of physical and emotional attention that even this is better than nothing, though even claiming such a point fills one with extreme discomfort. This is conflicting enough for the viewer, but it's when Charlie's friend arrives, armed with a shotgun, that the whole sequence becomes truly problematic. In a vile twist, Norman, played by Ken Hutchison, forces himself on Amy from the rear. Meanwhile David is in the middle of nowhere. He kills a duck and feels instant guilt for doing so, placing its limp, dead body back in a bush before heading off back to the village. Being a man to David, at this point, is not about firing a gun. He's a pacifist... for now at least.

She, violated and broken down, does not tell her husband what's happened. He, an intelligent man lacking in empathy for the woman he supposedly loves, seems to have an inkling that something has gone on. But it is not the rape of his wife which flicks the switch and turns David into a territorial beast, from a pacifist to a violent animal, but the moment the workers attack his home, his fortress, his castle, because he is hiding the town simpleton (played marvellously by David Warner) who has accidentally killed a local girl. In the final section of the film, David transforms from a mild mannered, slightly cowardly man of logic into a feral barbarian, who will do anything and everything to protect his home, his domicile, his ethics, the simple man who is now his responsibility, and, perhaps most importantly of all on a visceral and animalistic level, his woman. The brutal final chapter is unexpected on first viewing; not so much that David has become violent, but because he seems to be enjoying killing the men so much. Indeed, he quietly delights in the slayings, and in a haunting moment appears almost peaceful as he beats one of the intruders to death. As the Scottish bag pipe music blasts from the hi-fi speakers, David is clear a war is being fought, and he is not going to leave the house until he is the last man standing.

Hoffman gives a tremendous performance. In the first part of the film he is so emotionless and distant that one could mistake his jarring movements to be the hallmarks of an awkward, clueless performance. But David is so uncomfortable that Hoffman has to act this way in order to establish him as the set-apart academic, desperately stiff but hopelessly trying his best to loosen up with his wife and appeal to the heavy drinking locals. It is in the end though that Hoffman's performance comes full circle and makes true sense; it's in his glazed over eyes behind the broken glasses, his slightly floating movements, his beast-like protection of his domain. He becomes utterly wild, and it's a transformation done so subtly, and with such skill, that it seems inevitable while also being hugely shocking.

Hoffman had been in violent films before, but he had never taken such glee in acting out violence. In Little Big Man, he was forced into violence to survive, and seemed to detest his actions. Straw Dogs was different, but it was the conflicting image of a pacifist turned into a primitive that convinced him to take a part that had been turned down by such actors as Jack Nicholson and Donald Sutherland. In Straw Dogs, this mild mannered mathematician is never happier or more at ease than when pulverising his opponents. To get into the spirit, Dustin asked for fruit he could practice kicking and hitting with implements until they exploded, so he could get grasp David's new found love of destruction. He couldn't imagine enjoying smashing a skull, Hoffman later explained, but a piece of fruit was a different matter.

As staggering as Hoffman's work in the picture is, in many ways the film belongs to Susan George, who delivers a breathtaking and complex effort as a woman torn between conflicting emotions. The strange combination of sexual manipulation and child like innocence she embodies is superbly pulled off, and throughout the film she delivers lines, gestures and even subtle looks that not only affect the situation, but her whole life in general; and cleverly, it seems as if Amy, so apparently naive, is totally unaware of the power of her sexuality. It's not a comfortable area to explore and Straw Dogs is indeed often a very unpleasant film, but it also illustrates the power of the female, the ape-like attitude of the male and the darkness all around us, ready to explode if dynamics are knocked off kilter.

The film was a modest hit but became a notorious shocker, banned on home video for decades in the UK and reserved for a shelf of extreme cinema alongside Ken Russell's The Devils and A Clockwork Orange, both of which were also released in 1971 alongside Straw Dogs. Reviews were often harsh, reviewers clearly troubled by the film's message.

Roger Ebert gave it 2 stars, calling it a "major disappointment in which Peckinpah's theories about violence seem to have regressed to a sort of 19th-Century mixture of Kipling and machismo. What conclusions are we supposed to draw? That Hoffman achieved defeat in victory? That Peckinpah believes in the concept of a Just War? That drink drives men to the grave? The most offensive thing about the movie is its hypocrisy; it is totally committed to the pornography of violence, but lays on the moral outrage with a shovel. The perfect criticism of Straw Dogs already has been made. It is The Wild Bunch."

It's perfectly understandable of course that people would have a major problem with the twisted moralising of Straw Dogs. What is not clear is whether we are supposed to be OK with David's violence, see it as a justified defence against the scum outside trying to get in, or denounce him for sinking to their level. Kill or be killed is the attitude, but the fact that David stands up to them not for the rape of his wife but for the village idiot makes it a muddled and troubling choice. And this, perversely, is what makes Straw Dogs so effective. It plays with the mind, makes one think and even question our own views on violence. If you are like me, quietly delighted by the justice in the moment when David puts Charlie's head into an animal trap, then Straw Dogs has achieved something remarkable and twisted. To Peckinpah, justice is personal, and it lays in the baton, the club, the sword, and here most predominantly, the gun, no matter who's firing it at whom. One cannot simply "enjoy" Straw Dogs, but be challenged by it. In the end, when the blood is dripping down the walls and the glass is shattered, you don't so much feel like a mere observer, but a participant in the fight. And that is what makes it so powerful.

"I Say A Lot of Words..."

Dustin Hoffman As Lenny Bruce

After several odd ball choices and films that were conceived to be misfires, Dustin Hoffman delivered a performance that matched his two widely recognised tour de force roles of the late sixties, in The Graduate and Midnight Cowboy, with his portrayal of doomed stand up comedian Lenny Bruce in Bob Fosse's groundbreaking and utterly captivating Lenny.

For Dustin, it was a challenge, perhaps his biggest yet. For one, he was for the first time playing a real person, someone he had never met but who had a rich legacy he was all too aware of. In preparation he researched Lenny's life for a year, interviewing family members and friends obsessively. Though technically prepared in many ways, he still found the task of portraying Bruce, essentially the comedian's comedian, hugely daunting.

Hoffman was famously intense during filming and got so into the role of the ill fated and tortured comic icon that it was often confusing for those on set just who they were speaking to - was it Hoffman or Bruce? When Rolling Stone Magazine covered the making of the film, they were allowed access into Hoffman's methods. "For Hoffman," they wrote, "playing the part of Lenny Bruce is the most difficult thing he has ever done. It rips at him and tears at him and eats up the bulk of his humour, leaving him edgy and obsessive about his work. There are moments when he looks a decade older than his 36 years. Sometimes the cameras have to be halted —entire seconds when he drifts out of Lenny and into Dustin, when his eyes go wild with confusion and fatigue and bitterness."

The report speaks of tired crew members, a tyrannical Fosse, fresh off the success of Cabaret, and most descriptively of all, a crotchety Hoffman, foreseeing the end of man due to pollution ("We got ten years to sort the world out" he wisely predicts, much to the irritation of the scribe) and so wrapped up in the gruelling shoot and his temporary life as Lenny Bruce it seems as if he's ready to perform the deed of his Harry Kellerman character and jump off a building, if only to spare himself of this horrific experience.

The film itself, as it happens, is a masterpiece, an unpleasant glimpse into Lenny Bruce's seedy world, but a masterpiece all the same and one which was definitely worth Hoffman's intense suffering. The film is presented as a stylised biopic, with his wife Honey Bruce (played by Valerie Perrine) telling an off camera documentary filmmaker about life with her dead husband, intercut with their time together, his rise as a comic, his descent into self destructive drug addiction and ultimately his sleazy demise of a morphine overdose in 1966. It's unashamedly bleak, makes no apologies for its relentless manner and is absolutely gripping from the first frame to the last.

Though a film is the collected work of hundreds, often thousands of people, and there are certainly a lot of folk to thank and pat on the back for the success of this enduring movie, one can get it down to a handful. Fosse is, of course, excellent as director, a guiding light combining documentary with more conventional techniques, so we feel we are watching mainstream entertainment, a straight forward documentary and something altogether more different and fresh at the same time. In its presentation, Lenny could perhaps be seen as the first modern biopic, and one sees its influence in countless films from the past few decades, where documentary and film are seamlessly combined together, not as mere spoof or mockumentary, but for a more rounded, multi dimensional glimpse into the life of a real life person. Credit must also go to Julian Barry for the adaptation of his own book, a warts and all head-on dive into the world of Lenny Bruce, through his trials and tribulations, unflinchingly honest in its depiction of a tragically doomed man.

Then there are the performances. As Honey Bruce, Perrine is fantastic, rightfully winning the Best Actress Award at Cannes Film Festival, yet perhaps more deserving of the Oscar than that year's winner, Ellen Burstyn for Alice Doesn't Live here Anymore. The word fearless is thrown around quite a lot these days, but that is a word which can perfectly describe Perrine's portrayal of Bruce's wife, a complex and complicated woman. I can think of very few performances from the 1970s, effectively the decade of the male anti hero, where a woman was given the chance to be so full-on, daring and dynamic. Perrine takes the opportunity in both hands and runs with it. It's a staggeringly good effort.

Which brings me to Dustin Hoffman, who again, despite it becoming a familiar phrase at this point when assessing Hoffman's remarkable run of early movies, not only portrays Bruce in all his mythical qualities, but becomes him. He is still Hoffman of course, injecting as much as himself into the part and indeed learning from it in the process, but he channels Bruce so well that, during stand up performances especially, the film becomes documentation. He brings Bruce's unashamedly controversial and revolutionary material to life and, unsurprisingly considering the humour he had put into past films, is very funny too. But it's off stage where Hoffman is most impressive, and it's off stage as it happens that Lenny Bruce is not funny at all, but a very troubled, often twisted character, bent on self destruction and unable to avoid his own terrible fate. Dustin paints a sad picture of Bruce and portrays his fall from grace with precision, looking every inch the desperate addict whose behaviour and choice of outrageous material means he is subjected to repeated arrests, night club bans and court cases, the latter of which obsesses him so much he takes to reciting their transcripts on stage, thus alienating what fan base he has left. Hoffman chronicles his outrageous ascent and eventual plummet with perfection.

Critics were challenged by the film, clearly because they had rarely seen one combine so many elements together in order to tell its story. The New York Times were most impressed with Hoffman's on-stage scenes, and it was for the inclusion of them that they could overlook what they saw to be the film's flaws. "Lenny," they wrote, "looks to be about three-fourths dramatized biography and one-fourth recreated stage performances. These scenes trace Lenny's progression from the early nineteen-fifties, when he was a strip-joint to Lenny's last exhausted years, when, after successive police busts for drugs and obscenity, he had reduced his nightclub act to obsessive readings from the court records. This one-fourth of the film is so brilliant—and so brilliantly acted by Dustin Hoffman—that it helps cool one's impatience with the rest of the film, which is much more fancily edited and photographed but no more profound than those old movie biographies Jack L. Warner used to grind out about people like George Gershwin, Mark Twain and Dr. Ehrlich."

Roger Ebert was also irritated by the style of the film. "If the film Lenny works as fiction," he wrote, "that's all we have the right to expect. The problem is that it doesn't. Bob Fosse, who captured a time and form of show business so memorably in Cabaret, tries this time for a quasi-documentary style that gets in the way of his, and Lenny's, material. And Dustin Hoffman, good as he is in the title role, is never quite permitted to put together an organic, three-dimensional character. Dustin Hoffman does a good job of giving us a Lenny Bruce we can believe. He doesn't imitate the historical Bruce so much as create a new Lenny -- bitter, knife-edged and driven."

One flaw could be that the film likes the idea of Bruce being driven to self destruction by the repeated police harassment, when in fact he was already a doomed man before the stage antics brought him the wrong kind of attention. Yes the court cases and limitations put upon his act by the law did damage his life, but his destiny was already written by then. Dustin Hoffman said in an interview with Michael Parkinson that Bruce was going to meet his end this way no matter what course his life took, whether he'd become a famous stand up comedian or not. "He used drugs," he bluntly explained, and one sees his point. If someone has an addictive personality, they will feed that addiction any way they can. For Bruce it was with drink and drugs. Did his own material serve to kill him, or did it simply aid him in his inevitable pushing of the self destruct button? It was not the court cases that drove Lenny on to Heroin, though they can't have helped with his self abuse. Bruce was that most tragic of things, a man who was destined to give in to his demons.

This aside, Fosse's Lenny is a tremendously watchable film, driven by a sharp script, an interesting subject explored from multiple viewpoints and performances so rarely rivalled. Much more than a biopic, it's an experience, a harrowing one at that, and our demented tour guide is Dustin Hoffman in one of the most towering performances of his career.

"Is it Safe?"

Dustin Hoffman as the Marathon Man

The same year Dustin had starred with Robert Redford in the seminal All the President's Men, he made another film which stuck out and captured the interest of the movie going public. The great thing about Marathon Man is that it does not claim to be more than one would expect it to be, even though one can happily agree that it is infinitely richer than that. Its original theatrical poster was tag lined, quite simply, "a thriller", sparing us the cheesy slogans the filmmakers could have easily rammed down our throats, clichés and all. But Marathon Man is not just "a thriller", it's one of the greatest in the history of the genre, and beneath its tactics of suspense and tension is a wholly more evil subtext.

The film gave Dustin Hoffman another chance to work with his Midnight Cowboy collaborator, the brilliant British director John Schlesinger, and perhaps more importantly the opportunity to take centre stage in a mainstream action thriller. But as I wrote above, Marathon Man is not a standard entry in the genre. The thriller has long been a rich breed of film, but Marathon Man takes the formula one step further, rarely falling back on familiarities but instead continuously surprising, often stunning the viewer with each new unexpected plot twist. Writer William Goldman, upon whose book the film is based, once said he had a fear of boring his audience. With

Marathon Man, he avoided that risk by ensuring there wasn't time to get bored.

Hoffman plays a mature student named Babe Levy, an enthusiastic runner who wants to follow in his father's footsteps, an academic researcher who killed himself during the Communist witch hunt era. As we are introduced into Babe's daily routine, we also meet his brother, Henry (Roy Schneider), a government agent posing as an oil executive. He is currently involved in couriering diamonds for an ageing Nazi, Dr Szell (Lawrence Olivier), known as The White Angel. Szell is hiding out in South America, living off a trove of diamonds he robbed from Jews at Auschwitz. When his brother is killed on the way back from collecting some diamonds in New York, Szell wants to cover up the whole incident by killing all involved, including the courier. When Henry learns they are after him, he journeys to New York, visiting his brother Babe while investigating the diamond incident. Henry is suspicious of Babe's current girlfriend, Elsa (Marthe Keller), a Swiss immigrant who he believes may be working for Szell. When Henry is killed, Babe finds himself tangled up in the Szell affair, first kidnapped from his apartment, then brutalised and tortured by Szell, before escaping his clutches and realising the only way out of this ordeal is by standing up for himself.

William Goldman was paid a healthy half million for adapting his book to the screen, and he does so with such carefulness that nothing is lost in the transition. Producer Robert Evans was famously excited by the story itself, saying, "The book reads like the movie-movie of all time. I regard it as a cheap investment because you don't often find books that translate into film. This is the best thing I've read since The Godfather. It could go all the way – if we don't foul it up in the making."

Evans had a lot to be excited about. This wasn't just an action pot boiler, it was multi layered with various themes running through it that added weight and poignancy. It was a film about two very different brothers, one running away from his own past and being forced to face up to it in the end. The allusions to the holocaust were very brave for the time, especially in the genre. Importantly though the Nazis were not used flippantly, not merely villains put in for the sake of sensationalism. They stood for a more terrifying badness, a metaphor for man at his most evil.

What Goldman crafted was a tight, fast moving, extremely engaging and unpredictable script, crammed full of thrilling sequences, double bluffs and awe inspiring moments which send genuine shivers down the spine. The script is complimented of course by Schlesinger's excellent direction. Seven years earlier, when he made Midnight Cowboy, he had been a newcomer to the States. As one can see by the often over-artsy direction in the earlier Hoffman collaboration, it seems that his excited outsider's eye had calmed down by the time Marathon Man arrived on his lap, and he eases himself into the pace smoothly. The flashback scenes of Babe's childhood involving his deceased father do bring to mind Joe Buck's recollections in Midnight Cowboy, but otherwise the film is like fresh new ground for the highly talented Schlesinger, who naturally adapts his style perfectly to these deceptive, paranoiac surroundings.

"I hadn't done a thriller up to that point, and I loved doing it," Schlesinger told the Hollywood Interview. "I got very hooked on making suspense pieces after that. It's a game you play with the audience that's unlike any other kind of filmmaking."

In the title role, Hoffman is dazzling. At first he is a mystery to us, this compulsive runner who's finally deciding to go back to school and pursue what he feels is his destiny. He is slowly unravelled, with flashback and modern scenes, to be a man who runs for a reason. But he cannot run forever, not from himself or his past. If it takes a demon like Szell, a demon from all our pasts, a sadistic Nazi who brings forth horrific memories of the Holocaust, then so be it. If he's going to become a man, he may as well face true horror in the process.

Hoffman got himself in proper shape for the film, running everyday and working on a more athletic physique. This wasn't just to satisfy his method acting obsessions; it was also vital and necessary for the part, for Dustin not only had to look like a runner, he had to do a hell of a lot of running in the course of the film. He is perfect as the mild mannered, slightly odd outsider, called "the creep" by his neighbours, but he is even more convincing when he is suddenly and unexpectedly fighting for his life against the villain of all villains. His transformation is totally believable, rather like Straw Dog's David, even when the former shrinking violet stands with gun in hand at the end of the movie, aiming the barrel at the White Angel himself. It's another brilliant performance.

Which brings us to Laurence Olivier, who delivers a spellbinding and quietly terrifying effort as Szell, a devil on earth and man of pure evil who contrasts himself against Hoffman's boyish innocence marvellously. There were famous rumours that Hoffman and Olivier clashed over acting styles, but in fact they got along rather well.

When Hoffman stayed awake one night before filming in order to look suitably exhausted, Olivier uttered the immortal words, "my dear boy, why don't you try acting?" Hoffman later added to this story that the reason he was up all night was because he was partying at Studio 54, and insisted that he and the legendary Shakespearean were merely engaging in playful banter with each other. Whatever the truth is, both men deliver some of their finest on-screen work, regardless of whether method or straight forward acting was the right or wrong way.

Schlesinger himself saw the conflict of styles a different way. He told the Hollywood Interview, "I think that Olivier didn't want to improvise and Hoffman did. And it's true, Olivier's line Why doesn't he just act? that he said to me, not Hoffman, happened, because Hoffman was trying various acting techniques to appear out-of-it during the dental scenes. When I looked at the dailies I realized there was no reaction from Hoffman's eyes, so I had to completely reshoot all the close-ups. That's when Olivier said to me, Why doesn't he just try acting?"

Marathon Man features one of the most notorious scenes in the history of film, the horrifying dental torture scene, with Olivier asking the chilling question "is it safe?" over and over, confusing Hoffman, before performing some unnecessary removals. Not only is it an unforgettable scene, it's enough to put anyone off going to the dentists for the rest of their life.

It proved to be a critical and commercial hit, making 30 million at the box office in its year of release and earning rave reviews. Even in bad notices, Hoffman was praised for his acting. Newsweek called him "excellent" and Saturday Review said that "Hoffman's performance is perfection for the young man." Time Magazine also said it was one of his best performances to date.

Roger Ebert was slightly critical of the film, though only because he felt it had untidiness in the plot. "If holes in plots bother you," he wrote, "Marathon Man will be maddening. But as well-crafted escapist entertainment, as a diabolical thriller, the movie works with relentless skill."

Pauline Kael, never a big Hoffman fan to be honest, was among the harshest critics, famously calling it a "Jewish revenge fantasy" and criticising the violence. In the New Yorker she wrote, "Running around with cut nerves gives Hoffman more of an excuse for that gasping sound," before admitting that it was a perfect performance without a bum note.

Many recall Marathon Man for its infamous tooth scene, but really the whole film is a master class in how to execute a good escapist thriller. But the key to the power of this film is that it isn't all about escape, it's also about accepting and standing up to the past, not just for ourselves but for the whole of mankind.

The Value of Authenticity

Dustin Hoffman in Kramer Vs Kramer and Tootsie

In the 1970s Hoffman was famous, or to some infamous, for his dedication to perfection, his refusal to settle for anything less than the best, and his knack of capturing realism, authenticity, no matter what it took to achieve it. Dustin knew he was difficult, but he saw it more as integrity. "We were all pretentious at the beginning," he admitted, while looking back on his younger days as an idealistic actor. "Being in your twenties is a time of pretension, your idealism makes you pretentious. It was the late '50s, early '60s, it was Bob Dylan, Allen Ginsberg. It was all about non-conformity. No one did commercials. We turned a lot of that stuff down. We were precious. Even being successful was considered selling out."

On film, Dustin insisted on depicting the truth, often to the suffering of those around him. Over a decade into his movie career, he was still picking heavy subject matter and striving to achieve the best he could in his films, without a moment of phoniness. But his way of working did not make him many friends.

No film about divorce and the split of a family has topped the subtle and tasteful, but ultimately more devastating heights of Kramer vs. Kramer, the landmark movie Hoffman made in 1979. Based on the book by Avery Corman, and adapted to the screen by Robert Benton, the impact the film has on the viewer, even to this day, is hard to define. It's so underdone, meaning that in the best possible way, that one cannot help but realise it would never be made like this if it were coming out tomorrow. A family drama about the implosion of a thought-to-be solid unit would require double the budget in modern cinema, and would certainly feature more sappy melodrama, more schmaltz and a boat load of dramatic fireworks, F words flying back and forth, an obligatory sex scene, every tear jerking cliché in the book, and a heightened, utterly unrealistic finale which would only insult the viewer's intelligence, whether they knew it or not. Kramer vs. Kramer however, achieves a goal without plunging to the sentimental depths one has seen countless times in films that have followed it. It's remarkably low key and more believable for it, so much more real and affecting for its sense of grounded reality, refusing to overcook or overdo the ingredients in the mix.

The film follows advertising executive Ted Kramer (Dustin Hoffman), a workaholic who enjoys life in the workplace and has failed to realise his wife Joanna (Meryl Streep) has not only fallen out of love with him, but out of love with their life together, and perhaps life itself. When he returns home from work one evening, wired up from a long and successful day at work, she tells him she is moving out, leaving him and their son Billy (Justin Henry) to search for herself and her own place in the world. Slowly, Ted must learn how to live with and take care of his son. Putting his all into the father-son relationship, a bond organically develops which hadn't previously been there; and sadly, it may not have ever formed had Joanna not left the nest, a fact which Ted is all too aware of.

They struggle at first but soon begin to bond. The boy misses his mother, who not only leaves but does not visit or contact the pair for almost a year. Billy becomes reliant on Ted, a father who becomes a daddy in the course of the picture. When Joanna returns to the scene, she files for divorce and fights for custody of the boy; to which Ted objects, seeing as he has raised Billy alone for the past year and they have made a life as a duo. When the custody case arrives, Ted intends to fight Joanna with everything he's got, despite an increasingly unstable work life and a plummet in his income, to keep Billy by his side.

Kramer vs. Kramer is directed without any unnecessary showiness by Robert Benton, taking on the form of a filmed play rather than a glossy Hollywood movie. The sets and locations are bland, very modern, and ensure that focus is kept on the characters and their interactions. The script is unfussy, and the cast are so natural in their parts that it seems like not only are they improvising and letting their dialogue run free, but they are literally being their characters and that they will continue to have lives long after the movie is over.

Hoffman, a lover of improvisation (developed or spontaneous) is at his best here in a role where he is walking a tricky tight rope. Had he stumbled, the film would have wound up an overly sentimental cheese fest. But Hoffman is so truthful to the situation that we begin to believe he cares as much about Billy as Ted Kramer does. As it happens, Dustin himself had recently been through a divorce and later admitted that doing the film was like a learning curve for him on how he could be a better father. Hoffman tends to learn from his characters, and though he injects himself within the role for believability, this is one of the occasions where one feels Hoffman and Kramer overlapping and even complimenting one another. It's a perfectly nuanced and excellently delivered master performance, and rightly won him his first Best Actor Oscar after numerous nominations.

In the much smaller role of Joanna, Meryl Streep is just as brilliant, though her cold and distant character ensures we warm to her much less. In fact it is down to the viewer's individual patience and understanding if we feel much for her at all, and it's the sort of female role one would not encounter in modern cinema, for fear of political incorrectness. Her strained relationship with Ted is expertly played, but was probably helped out by the fact that she and Hoffman had an uncomfortable working relationship on the film. Streep was originally cast as the neighbour, Margaret (which went to Jane Alexander in the end) but managed to get an audition for Joanna and won the part. Hoffman later said that Streep may have been aided in her raw, often painful performance by the recent death of her partner John Cazale. Whether true or not, there is an edge to Streep's performance that makes it near documentary in style.

The icy atmosphere between the pair on screen gives the film its jaggedness, and it's been reported that Dustin was deliberately off hand with Streep on set in order to get the results he was looking for. Streep later said that Dustin groped her breast the first time they met, perhaps in a bid to throw her off from the word go. There was a professional disagreement too; Streep wanted the audience to see Joanna in a more positive light while Hoffman preferred her to be viewed from a distance as an ice queen. In order to keep the friction up, Hoffman apparently insulted Streep on set and even taunted her about Cazale's death. One of the film's most famous scenes, when they meet up in the restaurant and he smashes the wine glass against the wall, narrowly missing Streep's face, was an improvisation which

Streep knew nothing of. (Watch it again and one can see the genuine shock on her face.) Streep also admitted, more recently, that Hoffman once slapped her in the face, pretty hard, during shooting one scene. Whether Hoffman's actions were right or wrong, they produced the kind of results that few actors could achieve.

Nothing in Kramer vs. Kramer, not a single line, gesture or scene, feels ingenuine. Every moment is believable, raw and painful, so much so that one feels disappointed when viewing another film of this type, for no movie dealing with this subject matter was able to capture the heart wrenching sadness of divorce, and the conflicting emotions surrounding one, quite like it. It seems a cliché to say, but we just don't see filmmaking of this kind anymore - not in the mainstream any way - and we probably never will again.

Hoffman's award aside, Kramer vs. Kramer won other Academy Awards, including Best Picture, and received rave reviews from every corner of the media. Roger Ebert wrote a glowing review, stating "Kramer vs. Kramer is a movie of good performances, and it had to be, because the performances can't rest on conventional melodrama. Dustin Hoffman's acting is about the best in his career, I think, and this movie should win him an Academy Award nomination and perhaps the Oscar. His performance as Ratso in Midnight Cowboy might strike some people as better than this one, but he had the advantage there of playing a colourful and eccentric character. This time he's just a guy in a three-piece suit, trying to figure out the next 24 hours."

Variety called it his best performance in years, adding "Hoffman runs the gamut of emotional responses while never losing contact with reality." And that final statement says it all I believe; not only about this particular role, but all of Hoffman's finest work. His performances are honest, genuine and often so real that they hurt. This is no exception and it's arguable if, Rain Man aside, he gave a performance that matched it for authenticity ever again.

Three years after his Oscar win, Hoffman appeared in another film which was close to his heart and he very much believed in. Tootsie now sits in the line of classic "dragging up" comedies, which starts with the seminal Some Like It Hot and goes on to the touching Mrs Doubtfire. Like the two afore mentioned films, the dragging up is merely a plot device in order for the character to reach a kind of peace with himself, in this case to learn about being a real man through knowing and understanding what it's like to live as a woman, the trials and challenges of being female.

Tootsie begins by showing us that out of work actor Michael Dorsey (played by Hoffman) is finding it hard to land roles because he's notoriously difficult. His agent, portrayed excellently by the film's director, Sydney Pollock, can't get him a part in anything. "No one wants to work with you!" he shouts in frustration. Out of sheer desperation, perhaps to prove a point that he really is a gifted actor, and also to raise funds to stage his friend's play (the friend and room mate is played by, quite wonderfully, Bill Murray), Dorsey becomes a woman, Dorothy Michaels, and tries out for the hottest role in New York, to play the new nurse on TV's most popular day time soap.

After landing the role, Michael/Dorothy is faced with various obstacles and predicaments. Firstly, he becomes a huge success, not as Michael of course, but as his female alter ego, gaining popularity, a fan base and wide celebrity. There are also cons to the situation. He begins to fall for his co star, played by Jessica Lange, developing a deep friendship. Though Dorsey wants her heart, he inadvertently becomes the object of her father's desire, a character played subtly by Charles Durning. Dorsey, in the end, knows there is only one way out of this situation; to hang up his dress and say goodbye to Dorothy Michaels, and show the world the new Michael Dorsey.

As a film project, Tootsie began in the hands of Robert Evans' brother, Charles, who thought about adapting the play Would I Lie to You? to the big screen. Screenwriter Dick Richards began work on the script and showed it to Dustin Hoffman, who loved it but wanted total artistic control over the project. With Evans as producer, Hoffman signed on the dotted line and they continued to work on the script for the next couple of years. Hoffman had just won the Best Actor award at the Oscars and was looking for the right follow up project, and he had his eyes intent on bringing Tootsie to life.

Hal Ashby was originally down as director but at the relatively late stage of November 1981 Sydney Pollack replaced him. Hoffman and Pollack famously clashed creatively on set. Pollack, Hoffman has since said, was very much a "director" in the old fashioned sense; he made the decisions and hoped his say was final. Seeing as Hoffman had been on board the project from its earliest development however, he wanted a more collaborative part in the making of the film, and in Dustin's words, Pollack was not a collaborator. They fought endlessly over details, mostly in the trailer on set before filming commenced, in order to reach a compromise. Hoffman hated having to do so, but at this stage it was too late to replace Pollack. Besides, he was already doing a great job, and Hoffman must have thought a lot of him, seeing as he suggested he also play the agent (he replaced Dabney Coleman, who Pollack cast as the soap's director instead). Hoffman was famously difficult on set, but his persistence and dedication paid off. What could easily have been a clichéd, run of the mill drag comedy was lifted to a whole new area. Dustin for one has never considered Tootsie a comedy, and though there are some laughs, it is more a drama about self discovery, an awakening, about finding oneself and an understanding with the people in your life.

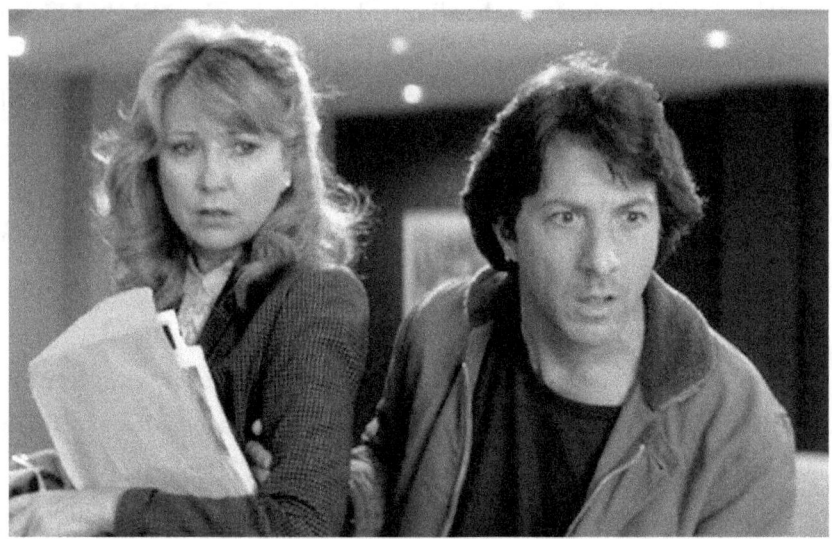

Teri Garr and Dustin Hoffman in Tootsie.

Tootsie may be slightly corny in some respects (not due to its age, though, for it was always on the cheesy side), but it's a film to see for the performances, all of which are extraordinarily good. Hoffman delivers another tour de force, a perfect performance which excels in every area. As Dorsey, he's the ultimate chauvinist, who views women as objects of desire but soon learns that there is an inner core to every woman which one must earn the right to see. As Dorothy, Hoffman is perfectly believable as the middle aged actress, a feminist unafraid to ruffle feathers as she stands her ground. The combination of both personas, and how Hoffman shines in both, is a testament to his abilities. Hoffman may be poking a bit of fun at his reputation, especially in the early segments when Dorsey is the comically difficult actor, but ultimately he is taking a journey within himself, understanding his flaws, his personal problems and shortcomings, before coming to a kind of conclusion about how he should interact with the people around him. The key line in the whole film comes at the end, when he says to Jessica Lange's character, "I've been a better man to you as a woman, than I ever was to a woman as a man." It's about understanding, putting oneself in the position of a woman to grasp what it is to be female. In the end, Dorsey has arrived, though as we see him and Lange stroll down the street getting to know one another in a new light, with Dorothy Michaels out of sight, we realise that Dorsey still has a lot of learning to do. But at least he's on his way. Even if the very end scene is not as convincing as everything that's come before, it least it's a conclusion.

Hoffman has often spoken of his disappointment that the makeup team couldn't make him a more attractive woman. "This is as good as it gets," they said, though Hoffman was happy when someone walked in during the play back of a screen test and asked "Who's the actress?"

Dustin also recalled having a conversation with his wife about how much he wanted the role. ""I said, I have to make this picture, and she said, Why? And I said, Because I think I am an interesting woman when I look at myself on screen. And I know that if I met myself at a party, I would never talk to that character because she doesn't fulfil physically the demands that we're brought up to think women have to have in order to ask them out. There's too many interesting women I have not had the experience to know in this life because I have been brainwashed,'"

Hoffman's Golden Globe winning efforts aside, the rest of the cast are top notch. Lange, in her Oscar bagging role, suitably downplays her soft and sensitive Julie, while Teri Garr, who arguably should have won the Oscar she was nominated for, is simply superb as Michael's ditzy, slightly hysterical acting friend/sometime girlfriend. Dabney Coleman is excellent as the strict Ron, Bill Murray quietly charismatic as Jeff the roommate and George Gaynes absolutely hilarious as the touchy-feely John Van Horn, Dr Brewster in the soap opera, who is known for enjoying his kiss scenes a little too much.

Still, this is Hoffman's show, when he was at the height of his powers and stubborn enough to know that his input would enrich the picture as a whole. Pollack may be holding the action together, but Hoffman's outstanding achievements are at the heart of this endlessly enjoyable classic.

Was It Really So Bad?

The Case for Ishtar, Legendary Box Office Bomb

Definitely the most savaged and undervalued film in Hoffman's long and varied filmography is Ishtar, the screwball comedy adventure movie written and directed by Elaine May. The hugely over budgeted farce came in at 51 million dollars, an obscene amount of money by anyone's standards, and managed to claw back 14 million. Reviews at the time of release were hostile, mocking, often cruel, and for many years Ishtar was deemed to be Hollywood's biggest flop and disaster. Today, though no Citizen Kane, its cult appeal has grown, mostly out of curiosity, and it is not without its fans. Admittedly when I first saw it, I wondered what all the negativity was about. Time is the true judge of art and though it hasn't blessed Ishtar like a fine wine, it's been rather kind to it.

The plot follows two American singer-songwriters who take up a Morrocan residency as performers but end up getting tangled up in the Cold War. The weirdest thing about Ishtar upon first sight is the odd ball casting; Warren Beatty is the rather slow one while Hoffman plays the sharp ladies' man. The concept seems inspired today, but it was this role reversal that attracted the first wave of criticism. It was followed quickly by a harsh ripping-to-shreds of everything else the film had to offer, which in critics' minds at the time was very little.

Ishtar began as a favour from Beatty to Elaine May. May had directed Beatty in Heaven Can Wait and had also helped out with his

Oscar winning 1981 epic Reds. When Ishtar came along he promised not only to produce the film but also take one of the leads in it. It was May who thought of Hoffman and though he was not won over by the script, he eventually agreed to sign up. The three main players were paid in advance (the sum was reportedly 12 million for all three) and the original budget was planned to be 27 million, though it wound up almost double that.

Filming was strained for political reasons and Morocco proved to be a disaster area for a major motion picture crew. The making of Ishtar is as often recalled as the film itself, and has gone down as one of the most disastrous shoots in history. May was shooting too much film, and as the problems mounted, Beatty turned to Hoffman and admitted this favour to May was turning into a big mistake. But they were in too deep now and the film had to be finished.

When they returned to New York to shoot scenes for the start of the film, Beatty had lost confidence in May and insisted each scene be directed twice, once her way, the other his. This added more money to the already ballooning budget. When the head of production was fired, he was briefly replaced by the famous David Puttman, who also quit after calling Dustin "the most malevolent person I have ever worked with."

When they retreated to the editing suite, it was revealed that there were 108 hours of footage to sort through, and most of it apparently awful. After more delays, it was finally released in May of 1987... and then came the storm.

Though this is a book primarily concerned with taking a fresh look at Hoffman's on screen work, and how it stands today in the modern context, one cannot ignore the critical mauling Ishtar was victim to at the time. Roger Ebert, in my view the greatest American film critic there has ever been, began his review at the time by getting straight to the point: "It's hard to play dumb. There's always the danger that a little fugitive intelligence will sneak out of a sideways glance and give the game away. The best that can be said for Ishtar is that Warren Beatty and Dustin Hoffman, two of the most intelligent actors of their generation, play dumb so successfully that on the basis of this film there's no evidence why they've made it in the movies. Ishtar is a truly dreadful film, a lifeless, massive, lumbering exercise in failed comedy. Elaine May has mounted a multimillion dollar expedition in search of a plot so thin that it hardly could support a five-minute TV sketch. And Beatty and Hoffman, good soldiers marching along on the trip, look as if they've had all wit and thought beaten out of them. This movie is a long, dry slog. It's not funny, it's not smart and it's interesting only in the way a traffic accident is interesting."

The Washington Post were similarly unimpressed, though they too seemed to be enjoying the chance to tear the movie apart. They called it "A mammoth dud, a catastrophe, a huge floundering stinker of biblical proportions -- that's what all the advance stories on Ishtar have prepared us for. In fact, it's not nearly so grand an achievement. Ishtar doesn't attempt enough to be considered a magnificent failure. It's something far less substantial; it's piddling -- a hangdog little comedy with not enough laughs."

The Post were also picking up on one of the film's central jokes, the irony of the casting, which they felt didn't really weigh up to much in the scheme of things. "One of the central jokes in the movie is that Beatty can't get girls," they wrote, "and, conversely, that

Hoffman can. But both performers here seem to be caught up in a kind of shrinking game. It's a pretty grim spectacle, watching these two middle-aged movie stars trying to out cute one another. Usually star performers do battle over salaries and close-ups and top billing. (That's why God made agents.) But here Hoffman and Beatty seem to fight over who gets to be second banana. Hoffman isn't bad in the film; unlike Beatty, he at least seems to be in there working to make the jokes pay off. But Hoffman isn't really right for this kind of role. He's too much of an actor. You can see that he doesn't have as much to engage him here as he might have in a more substantial role, and so all his energy is directed toward keeping himself in check - gearing down."

With Tootsie being Dustin's most recent cinematic offering, before he returned to the stage in the mid 80s for Death of a Salesman, Ishtar was his first film in five years. But it wasn't much of a comeback. Seen as a joke and a mega flop, Ishtar was the first serious dint in Hoffman's career, not so much a bump in the road but a mountain. Yet there were some critics who enjoyed it, with Vincent Canby maybe going a little too far by picking it out as one of his favourite films of the year.

Thirty two years on, is Ishtar really so bad? In my view, no. It's even engaging at times and though financially overblown for no real reason, it's good fun, utterly harmless and not without laughs. The performances, too, are rather good, and Hoffman is smart with the material he is given. He later told Charlie Rose that one of the aims of the film was to celebrate the keen amateur, the second rate artist who is validated by the fact he is loving what he's doing, and how that person can be more laudable than the first rate professional who has no passion. That is one of the factors which makes this unfairly mocked film rather sweet. At the end of the day, it's just a movie, and one that isn't that bad after all. Despite the feedback, Hoffman and Beatty remained satisfied with the film and even worked together again three years later on Dick Tracy.

These days it's something of a cult favourite. Some fans like it for ironic reasons but others have called it a genuinely good movie that received unfair criticism due to the back story of its production. In the New Yorker recently, writer Richard Brody called it a masterwork, while the Guardian wrote a lengthy reappraisal of it, which included statements like: "While Ishtar has not appreciated into a stealth masterpiece in the mould of Showgirls' long road to reappraisal, its stature as the definitive cinematic failure has been outed as undeserved. May's final film was flawed but idiosyncratically so, hardly the ruinous quagmire suggested by its legacy. It survives today as a curious artefact of film history, more fascinating than entertaining, deserving of study rather than popcorn."

They also saw the film's awful treatment by critics and industry insiders as classic sexism. They may have had a point. After all, May was never given a second chance at making a film, while Hoffman and Beatty cruised immediately on to big projects. "A significant footnote in the ongoing story of showbiz misogyny, a perfect storm of misjudgement made possible through called-in favours, Ishtar's place in its time and industry has more meaning and value than the content of the film itself. It's an odd orphan, not howlingly bad enough for ironic adoration at midnight screenings, but not competent enough for enshrinement in the canon. It survives today primarily as a testament to the audacity of Elaine May's ambition as a humorist, and a look at the potential future that showbiz wrongfully wrested from her. Far from a landmark, it's a part of Hollywood history all the same."

Sexual politics aside, Ishtar is not so-bad-it's-good, nor is it the underrated masterpiece a fan like Quentin Tarantino claims it to be. It's basically a run of the mill screwball comedy nicely played by two actors performing against type. It just happens it's also one of the least successful and most over budgeted films of all time.

"I'm An Excellent Driver..."

Dustin Hoffman As Raymond Babbit
in Rain Man

It's hard to imagine, in the modern commercial film world, that an actor would immediately be given a chance in a mainstream movie after a flop as disastrous as Ishtar. Granted, Hoffman had been a bankable (that dreaded word) name for a couple of decades at this point, but even so, he had been free enough to explore whatever role took his fancy regardless of its commerciality, or lack thereof. For every Little Big Man there was a curio like Alfredo, Alfredo; for every Marathon Man a Straight Time - and so on. After a wreck on the scale of Ishtar though, most actors would have laid low for a while. Hoffman however not only redeemed himself, but rose to a new kind of height, as far as his acting was concerned, that he had never reached before.

The film in question is Rain Man. It follows Tom Cruise as Charlie Babbitt, a car dealer struggling with loan payments. He's a typical product of the era, a flashy, arrogant yuppy seemingly lacking in empathy, with a caring girlfriend (played by the underrated Valeria Golino) who struggles with his obnoxious aloofness. When his father dies, Charlie travels to Ohio to go over the will, learning he is only going to be left a rare 1949 Buick. The rest of the 3 million dollars estate is going to a mystery figure, which he soon learns is his long lost brother, Raymond Babbit (Dustin Hoffman), a middle aged sufferer of autism residing, voluntarily, in a mental institution. Hoping to get what he feels is his deserved half of the money, Charlie convinces Raymond to come with him in the car, a vehicle Raymond remembers from his childhood, where they leave the grounds of the hospital and book into a hotel. Charlie does not realise however, how hard it will be to spend time with Raymond, a man religiously used to his rituals and routines. His impatience with his new found brother alienates Charlie's girlfriend, who exits the film and leaves the reunited siblings alone. Wanting the money but unable to negotiate a deal for himself, Charlie hopes to win custody of Raymond and take him home. Raymond, stubbornly dedicated to his needs, is unwilling to travel by plane for fear of crashing. Instead, they take a road trip across America, where Charlie slowly begins to develop a soft spot for his brother.

Bizarrely, the film project, developed by producer Roger Birnbaum, began as a concept with Bill Murray in Hoffman's role and Hoffman in Tom Cruise's role. Writer Barry Morrow wrote the script after meeting Kim Peek, a real life autistic. Thankfully, Hoffman shifted roles and the hottest new star of the 1980s, Cruise, was cast as the younger brother. When Rain Man was finally completed and released, it was a critical smash which eventually went on to become the highest grossing film of 1988, a success in the truest manner. But during filming, Hoffman and Cruise were unsure about the film and the work they were doing with director Barry Levinson. While they clearly enjoyed their chance to improvise (the hilarious fart in the phone booth scene was knocked up when Hoffman genuinely did fart during the shoot), Cruise and Hoffman referred to the film as "Two Schmucks in a Car."

For Levinson himself, it was about making a relationship between these two men that was not only believable but also engaging. "To fully realize these characters," he told Rolling Stone, "my idea was to ask, cinematically, what happens when Charlie talks to his autistic brother? He can't sell him, because no matter what he says or how he tries to con him, Raymond wants what he wants. Raymond never initiates a conversation. Raymond never looks at you when he talks. I've never seen a character like this one. Many audiences like gizmos, plot things, cops and all that kind of shit, in which I'm not interested. If I can show the autism for what it is and understand it – show the frustration and the humour – if I can make the relationship work with these two guys on the road, then that's enough for me."

Famously, Hoffman was so unsure about his work at one point that he was seriously considering quitting. Before the shoot he had delved head long into research, tirelessly observing autistic sufferers and studying their behaviour in documents and on video tape. When Hoffman arrived on set though, even after spending time with genuine autistic sufferers, he felt hopelessly ill prepared. "It was death," he recalled, "it was the worst work I have ever done. I said 'I can't do it.'" Hoffman even suggested getting Richard Dreyfus instead, but Levinson was adamant that Dustin was the right man for the part.

The key to the role for Dustin was an improvisational scene which came out of nowhere in the car, when he began to rant about his underwear, in character as Raymond. Levinson told Hoffman, "it looked like to me that you could have talked about your underwear forever," and it was then that Hoffman understood which angle to come from. "And I suddenly realised this character is in the now, and he is nowhere if he is not in the now. And I suddenly realized that I was playing off myself because I know something about obsession and I'm comfortable being obsessive. The rest of it just took care of itself."

Hoffman is, quite simply, staggering in the film. Even considering the earlier shape shifting roles, like Midnight Cowboy's Ratso and Little Big Man's Jack Crabb, this is the most drastic transformation of his film career. It is not a physical metamorphosis of course, but a psychological one, even spiritual. Hoffman's eyes, glazed over at all times, are elsewhere, and one believes Dustin is living and thinking as Raymond Babbit. Obviously the intense research he did for the part helped, but there is something on another level going on which is hard to define. As Hoffman said, it's more about being in the now and he is clearly in the moment as Babbit at all times, thinking in a different way in order to channel the character and believably portray the complexities of the condition.

As it happens, Cruise is just as impressive in his own way, though as it's not as showy or exotic a role as Hoffman's, one does not instantly see and recognise the complexity of the part. Reacting to Raymond, especially in a believably frustrated manner, must have been hard for Cruise to act out; but he gets under Charlie's skin quite brilliantly, and keeps the film warm, human and relatable from the word go. We might not like Charlie's impatience with Raymond, but we at least get it. And as he makes his way to understanding and even loving Raymond, he begins to understand himself and where he's been going wrong. He repairs the poor relationship with his late father by making a connection to Raymond. The real tragedy is of course that one wonders if Raymond is aware of the connection in the slightest, and will not emotionally side line his younger brother as soon as the picture ends. The finale of the film leaves this open to the viewer, rather cleverly I think, without putting a full stop at the climax.

Rain Man could have easily wound up an overly sentimental schmaltz fest, but Levinson avoids tenderness in favour of realism. The sound track for one refuses to opt for the clichéd string section, and though there are warm moments between the brothers (especially when Charlie learns that his childhood recollection of the almost mythical Rain Man was Raymond himself), we are never guided towards a way of feeling. We are not told to like Charlie; in fact, for the most part we are encouraged to dislike him. But we begin to sympathise with him, and see things from his viewpoint, the left-out son desperate for a meaningful connection with someone. That someone, as it happens, turns out to be Raymond. Levinson keeps the pace speedy so there is never a dull moment, and we are constantly hooked on the interactions and developments between the two siblings.

The film swept the Oscars, winning Best Film and, vitally, Best Actor for Hoffman, his second honouring from the Academy. Reviews were mostly positive, and though it opened slow, Rain Man earned 350 million dollars at the box office, a staggering amount for such an intimate film.

Rain Man got people thinking, critics included, and for the first time people were paying attention to conditions like autism on a serious level. It certainly brought up dilemmas for Roger Ebert, who began his review with the question, "Is it possible to have a relationship with an autistic person? Is it possible to have a relationship with a cat? I do not intend the comparison to be demeaning to the autistic; I am simply trying to get at something. I have useful relationships with both of my cats, and they are important to me. But I never know what the cats are thinking. That is precisely the situation that Charlie Babbitt (Tom Cruise) is faced with in Rain Man."

He went on to seriously praise Hoffman, writing that "few actors could get anywhere with this challenge, and fewer still could absorb and even entertain us with their performance, but Hoffman proves again that he almost seems to thrive on impossible acting challenges. You want taller? he asks in the audition scene in Tootsie. I can play taller. You want shorter? I can play shorter. You want a tomato? And he can play autistic. At the end of Rain Man, I felt a certain love for Raymond, the Hoffman character. I don't know quite how Hoffman got me to do it. He does not play cute, or lovable, or pathetic. He is matter-of-fact, straight down the middle, uninflected, unmoved, uncomprehending in all of his scenes - except when his routine is disrupted, when he grows disturbed until it is restored. And yet I could believe that the Cruise character was beginning to love him, because that was how I felt, too. I loved him for what he was, not for what he was not, or could not be."

Ebert is dead right. Raymond becomes one of cinema's most loveable characters throughout the course of the film, yet Hoffman's excellent performance is so much of an enigmatic mystery that it's hard to define how he actually did it. It is a flawless portrait of a man existing outside the parameters of what we consider rationality, impossible to reach on a one to one level but also impossible not to love. Like Charlie, we want to knock down the wall and connect with him, get past the glazed over eyes and see what's really going on his head. To make such a distant man, who's always a thousand miles away from the so called real worlds, seem so close and only just out of reach, is genius as far as acting is concerned. The film itself is certainly among the top five of Hoffman's career, but it's also in serious competition for featuring the finest performance Hoffman has ever given. Rain Man is a special film, and it's one which seems to grow in importance and impact with each passing year.

The Curious Nineties

A Decade of Ups and Downs

Though most of these essays focus on individual or paired performances, it seems fitting somehow to group all of Dustin Hoffman's output of the 1990s in one category. This was a rich and eccentric time period, which took him from kooky cameos to Oscar nominated roles. For me, it is also his last truly interesting decade. Since the 90s Hoffman has become one of those veteran legends, so used to giving in-depth character study performances in a vastly different industry that he's struggled to get to grips with the change in the tide. Indeed, he's a character actor, a product of the 60s and 70s movie revolution, stuck in a mainstream battlefield in which he simply cannot find his place.

The 90s, however, were different. Like his contemporaries, Jack Nicholson, Al Pacino and Robert De Niro among them, he found his footing and added a host of memorable parts to his rich gallery of faces. The first 90s film he appeared in was Dick Tracy. A massive hit film upon its release, Warren Beatty's arty, bold and daring adaptation of the classic comic book is largely overlooked these days, despite the fact it was one of the highest grossing movies of its era. At a time when comic book blockbusters were all the rage, and the likes of Tim Burton's Gothic reimagining of Batman were topping the box office charts, Beatty came up with the idea of bringing Chester Gould's classic cartoon strip to life on the big screen, and he did so with endlessly imaginative results.

As well as directing and producing, Beatty also stepped into the shoes of the crime fighting, yellow coated detective, taking on gangster boss Big Boy Caprice (Al Pacino) and his group of cronies. Madonna plays the seductive singer Breathless Mahoney, who Caprice steals from a rival mobster he kills off early in the film. She brings to the role an element of Marilyn Monroe, some well placed vintage glamour, only with the suggestion and innuendo shot way up the scale. The outfits too are certainly more revealing. She effortlessly glides in and out of the film, oozing total star charisma and is endlessly watchable whether she's seducing Tracy or singing one of the movie's catchy numbers.

There's a whole cast of dazzling stars throughout, from Dustin Hoffman's outrageously funny, reluctant informer Mumbles, to rival gangster James Caan. The only star names who are remotely recognisable as themselves are Beatty and Madonna, who were dating at the time. In many ways though, as good as Madonna is in her role, the film is dominated by a toweringly hilarious performance from Al Pacino, parodying his own Tony Montana/Scarface role to a tee. Still, Hoffman fans will be amused by his hilarious, bumbling cameo.

Another unfairly overlooked film from Hoffman's canon is 1991's Billy Bathgate, a crime thriller which features Dustin in one of his most menacing guises. If Hoffman's gallery of faces is short on one thing then it's villainous characters, though the ones that exist are definitely memorable. Consider, for instance, his twisted character in the later released Confidence, definitely the least savoury of all his roles and one that hardly ever gets picked out. The same can be said for his part in this, a pretty much forgotten gangster picture that might not be among his best films as a whole, but features some unforgettable scenes and a glittering cast who, though delivering showy performances, are effective in their roles.

Hoffman plays the vicious, merciless gangster Dutch Schultz, a nasty piece of work for sure, who takes on a young teenager who's living under the name Billy Bathgate (played blandly by Loren Dean) and shows him the ropes. Bruce Willis has a smaller role as a rival mobster, Bo Weinberg, who is murdered by Schultz, while Nicole Kidman plays Bo's girlfriend, who ends up in a relationship with Schultz.

Adapted from EL Doctorow's novel by the esteemed Tom Stoppard, the film is hardly a fast moving thrill ride but more about character and tension. Though it could never be called a gangster classic, it's engaging and unsettling, keeping the viewer guessing. Hoffman is brilliant, by far the stand out in the cast, and it's a shame so few people seem to be aware of his work in this one. Gruff voiced, rough and ready, it's almost (and I say almost) a cartoonish performance, the kind one would get from Cagney in the likes in the 1940s; but Dustin is smart enough to know that such a broad portrayal of a mobster, while brilliant in the golden age, would have been ludicrous in the early 1990s. He often walks a thin line, but ultimately comes out on top.

Unfortunately the reviews at the time were rather poor and the film was a massive flop, almost on the scale of Ishtar in fact, making only 15 million dollars back on its 48 million budget. (Where all the money went is anyone's guess to be honest.)

Roger Ebert thought it a nothing performance, writing "Dutch Schultz is played in the movie by Dustin Hoffman, in one of his rare dispensable performances. There is nothing here - absolutely nothing - that needed Dustin Hoffman to do it. The script shows him facing trial and imprisonment, with the law finally breathing down his neck. Rival gangsters are carving up his turf, and already fighting for the spoils they expect him to leave behind. Dustin Hoffman still hadn't found a person inside his suit as the movie was ending. Walking out of the movie, I was unable to answer two basic questions: What was it about? And, What did it want to say?"

Variety were also unimpressed, writing "Hoffman's performance is problematic. There is a stiffness that sets his impersonation apart from his best characterizations."

Buried in time, Billy Bathgate is worth digging out for a viewing, though repeated ones might not be so necessary. The same year it was released, Hoffman took part in a film that was by no means ignored. Director Steven Spielberg was on quite a roll at this stage in his career, and with classics like Jaws, Raiders of the Lost Ark and E.T. under his belt, he was already the most successful film director of his age. With Hook and the films that followed in the 1990s, his stature and commercial clout would only grow. Love him or hate him, at one stage he defined the mainstream blockbuster, and while his cinematic vision may have spawned a whole lot of junk from commercially minded hacks that came in his wake, much of his own output remains pure, good old fashioned entertainment, harmless fun for the whole family.

Hook, released in 1991 as the blockbuster began to take over the serious picture, continued Spielberg in his extravagant pursuit of ticking every box, being liked by as many people as possible and raking in as much box office takings as he could. This ludicrous but fun picture, scripted by Jim V Hart and Mala Marmo, runs on the rather daft premise of Peter Pan as a grown up, who's left Neverland long ago, forgotten about his old friends and enemies in that magical land and become a lawyer. When visiting his wife's grandmother, Wendy Darling, the family get an unexpected visit from the villains of Neverland, who kidnap his two children. Forced to face up to a past he has not only left behind but also forgotten, the middle aged Pan journeys to Neverland to save his kids, where he must battle his old nemesis, Captain Hook.

Though full of embarrassing moments and cheesy as a block of stilton, there is a lot to enjoy about Hook. For one, Robin Williams is fabulous as the ageing Pan, a stuffy, strung up Peter Banning, though does become slightly irritating as he regresses to his childhood persona. Bob Hoskins is wonderful as Hook's side man, Smee, and there are other fine performances throughout, such as Dick Tracy child actor Charlie Korsmo. The true star of the show however, special effects aside, is Dustin Hoffman in his towering depiction of the nasty, bloodthirsty, heartless but ultimately hilarious Captain Hook. Hoffman has given this potentially one dimensional villain multiple sides; he's nasty but also sensitive, arrogant but self pitying, and as it turns out in one hilarious scene, so self doubting that he's ready to commit suicide. Hoffman is so good as Hook that the viewer finds themselves - or me at least - waiting for his return to the screen. So corny and annoying are many of the scenes with Pan being re-trained by the Lost Boys that one wonders what the film would have been like without Hoffman, and just how unwatchable it might have wound up. Is Hoffman the film's saving grace? In my view, yes.

That said, this is a family film and as a child I loved it, and never found it remotely irritating. As an adult, I see it differently, though re-watching it is by no means unpleasant, mainly due to Hoffman's work. There is a lack of cynicism to it, and also the autobiographical element, for Spielberg at least, makes the film seem that little bit more genuine and heartfelt than your average money-maker. As the ageing Pan is a workaholic who sidelines his own family, Spielberg saw direct parallels to his own dad, and a childhood he spent being ignored by his work driven father. For me, and many others too, watching a film such as Hook is like revisiting our own childhood and one can easily get wrapped up in its magical silliness, as flawed as it may be in many areas. Still, for Hoffman alone it's a treat worth taking another taste of.

After the smash success of Hook, Hoffman had another commercial clunker added to his CV in the form of Accidental Hero (1992), titled simply Hero in the US, though again, like Billy Bathgate and Ishtar, it wasn't really as bad as it was made to be. Like the two afore mentioned films however, it too had a massively over the top budget, and once again it was hard to see just where the money (in this case a whopping 40 odd million!) had gone.

Directed by the great Stephen Frears, who had just made The Grifters, the film follows Hoffman as Bernie, a shady pickpocket who saves a plane load of people after a crash, including TV reporter Gale Gayley, played by Geena Davis. Given he was entering the burning wreckage to rob the passengers, Bernie is unaware that the press are looking for the angel of flight 104; enter homeless Vietnam vet Andy

Garcia who steps up and receives not only a million dollar reward but instant fame and adoration. Meanwhile, no one believes the real hero, the sleazy Bernie, and his far fetched tale.

Accidental Hero is a typical film of its time; a mainstream comedy drama with a totally far fetched and impossible plot, so well acted and nicely directed that it's impossible to put it down because it makes for such good entertainment. Though the film gets more and more ridiculous as it goes along, it's irresistible all the same, thanks mostly to the wonderful performances. Garcia is good, Davis shines as usual, but again, predictably, it's Hoffman who delivers the most multi layered performance, despite it still being on the side of broad caricature. Again, it's one of those seedy roles, like Ratso, which he so naturally excels in. As a film it raises a few issues about judging a book by its cover, about natural and understandable prejudices that, no matter how much we don't like them, will always exist. It also tells us that the hero is not always the perfect saviour he is held up to be.

Reviews were good, yet many publications were reluctant to pick out Hoffman as the finest player. New York Times, for instance, lauded Davis' work. "Hero is a big, expensive-looking, quite harmless Hollywood comedy that is finally far more enjoyable than it has any right to be, largely because of Dustin Hoffman, Andy Garcia and Geena Davis, but most of all because of Ms. Davis... what really counts is her angularly comic presence. She's as cheering and surprising as the sight of a very tall lollipop careering around on Rollerblades."

Roger Ebert was not a huge fan of the film, and thought Hoffman's performance started good and eventually went off the deep end. "Hoffman's performance is one of the problems. He's good in the setup scenes," wrote Ebert. "Then his character gets wordy and there are scenes which make every point twice. His behaviour during the actual rescue is all self-indulgent overacting; there's no contact with psychological possibility... he gets sentimental, and there are deadly scenes with his kid that had me squirming with impatience. All of this is joined to Hoffman's patented shuffling little-guy walk, which I first saw onstage in his Death of a Salesman, where it worked, but which he has now used in at least one movie too many. He's going for pathos with a character who should be a smart-aleck."

Whether Hoffman's performance is slightly off or not (I personally liked it), Hero is a nice old fashioned 90s movie that would never get made today, at least not in this fashion. Oh nostalgia....

The 1990s really were the decade of the blockbuster, and by that I mean the kind that took you on a ride. Yes, blockbusters had come before then, and they would certainly flood the film market afterwards, but in the 1990s, with the introduction of CGI, the epic, monstrously budgeted popcorn flick was at its height. This was the age when every other film was either an action adventure film, a tense, dramatically soundtracked thriller, or an epic disaster movie. Outbreak, directed by Wolfgang Petersen and released in 1995, was from the latter category. With a budget of 50 million dollars, thankfully for all involved, Hoffman included, it was a sizeable hit, making almost four times its budget back in the year it was unleashed to a terrified but highly entertained public.

The film follows the spread of the deadly Motaba virus, on its way from Africa, which is hosted by a small capuchin monkey. The mission is to stop the spread of this terrible disease before it wipes out all of western civilisation. On the case, thankfully, are virologist Colonel Sam Daniels, played with sturdy authority by Dustin

Hoffman, his ex wife, Robert Keough, portrayed by 90s staple Rene Russo, and a host of other experts.

Outbreak is a fast moving, exciting thrill ride, and it would take someone extremely repulsed by blockbusters of any kind to not enjoy it. Where Outbreak excels is in its build up, the way it mounts tension from the start and steadily informs us just how hazardous this virus really is. Character development is vital too, for we genuinely care for and like the people that are put up on the screen. Too many modern blockbusters, many of which are budgeted at four times the amount it cost to make Outbreak, dive straight on into action within the first minute, leaving little or no time for character, not to mention subtlety of any kind, meaning we immediately do not care what happens. Outbreak may be familiar, formulaic and sticking to a safe set of Hollywood rules, but it works within its boundaries very well and keeps the viewer hooked. This is not a mindless bombardment of explosions, fist fights and head spinningly naff CGI effects, it's a gripping drama enclosed within an enthralling thriller, where time is running out and we definitely know about it.

It helps of course that the acting is very good. Hoffman isn't outstanding, but then again his role does not require anything truly breathtaking, and he's a strong, reliable lead, proving he really could adapt his acting style to suit any genre or backdrop. Russo is great too, but for me the most effective performance comes from Donald Sutherland as the nasty General McClintock, while Cuba Gooding Jr, just before his Oscar win for Jerry Maguire, is also a stand out.

Reviews were mixed in some quarters, but serious critics like Roger Ebert could see it was a master class in its genre, calling it "one of the great scare stories of our time" and "a clever, daunting thriller.

Outbreak is the kind of movie you enjoy even while you observe yourself being manipulated. The Hoffman character has been recycled out of dozens of other movies... But the roles are well written and acted. I am not sure I believed the helicopter chase sequence in Outbreak, and I am sure I didn't believe the standoff between a helicopter and a bomber. But by then the movie had cleverly aligned its personal, military, medical and scientific plots into four simultaneous countdowns, and I was hooked."

In a style fitting to his legacy, Hoffman followed up the huge budgeted Outbreak with a small, intimate drama, based on David Mamet's acclaimed play, American Buffalo. It could have not been more different than his previous outing, this claustrophobic character piece. It concerns Donny (Dennis Franz), owner of a downtown junk shop in the least aesthetically pleasing neighbourhood imaginable. Sean Nelson plays Bobby, a younger man who hangs around the shop, and Hoffman is Teach, a seedy lay about, who never seems to want to go home. One day he comes up with a plan, to rob a man's safe thought to contain rare coins. The robbery, however, does not exactly go to plan.

American Buffalo first burst on to the theatre in the mid 1970s, making Mamet a name to watch. In the years that followed he continued to write acclaimed plays like Glengarry Glen Ross and Speed the Plow, while he scripted such films as The Untouchables, We're No Angels and The Postman Always Rings Twice. American Buffalo, one of Mamet's least cinematically inclined plays, was first developed for the screen with his Glengarry Glen Ross star Al Pacino tipped for Teach, the very part he had won rave reviews for on stage. When Pacino did not respond quickly enough, Dustin Hoffman was offered the role instead. I must say, as good as Pacino would have been (think of his Levine in the film version of Glengarry Glen Ross), Hoffman is suitably dynamic. His Teach is a sleazy, grubby individual with shades of Ratso Rizzo about him. Upon first viewing, many years ago now, I was instantly struck by the power of his presence and the sheer exuberance he harboured. Indeed, the film does come to life whenever he appears, and I would confidently rank it among his finest performances in the last thirty years, even if the critics who claimed he was forcing it a bit might be valid in their criticisms.

American Buffalo hardly set the world alight however and seemed to come and go without much fanfare. Reviews were mixed. The Daily Telegraph were critical of both Hoffman's acting and the film itself, writing "Hoffman, performing in 'street' mode, complete with long greasy hair, never allows you to forget that he's reciting lines. Eventually the hypnotic repetitiveness of the language and the total lack of action did their work, and the dreaded Sandman, who hovers constantly at the shoulder of all film reviewers, paid me one of his visits."

Roger Ebert was also critical of Hoffman, stating "Dustin Hoffman somehow seems to be trying too hard, to be making too much of an effort to think his thoughts and speak them. His Teach doesn't seem in on the joke, which is that nothing much is going to happen and Teach sort of knows that."

Hoffman then took a smaller role in Sleepers (also 1996). Adapted from Lorenzo Carcaterra's gripping novel (supposedly based on truth, although many have doubted the author's claims), Sleepers tells the story of a group of boys sent to a detention centre after nearly killing a man when a prank goes horribly wrong. There they are brutally raped and beaten by the guards, most cruelly by the sadistic Kevin Bacon. Years later, the boys have grown into men and each live very different lives. Now feared gang members, two of the grown up boys, Tommy and John (played by Billy Crudup and Ron Eldard) come across their former abuser in a bar and shoot him dead in a bloody fashion. Brad Pitt plays the adult Michael, an attorney who is assigned to oppose his old friends in the court, in a bid to sabotage the case in their favour. The case that follows is a harrowing watch, but finally justice will be served, albeit in a bittersweet fashion.

Sleepers is a sturdy, powerful film which relies on a strong cast, all of whom give brilliant performances. But it does offer some muddled moral questioning. The fact that Tommy and John have clearly already murdered and got away with it, and are little more than monsters created by their horrific past, presents us with a worrying feeling, when we realise we want them to get away with it. The fact they are both destined for oblivion anyway, and neither live to the age of 30 as we are told at the end of the film, makes the whole labouring case somewhat futile, highlighting the sheer tragedy and long lasting negative effects on an abused individual. Even when they win, Brad Pitt's character is still disappointed.

Providing the conscience for the boys, as children and men, and the backbone of the whole film in fact, is the reliable Father Bobby, played with charm and believability by a warm Robert De Niro. Some of the film's most subtle and therefore powerful moments involve De Niro, in particular the scene where he has no real option but to lie for the two killers in the court. Just look at his eyes when he takes a look at the Holy Bible and places his weary hand over it, swearing the oath. It sends a shiver down the spine, but De Niro uses such fine brush strokes that we could barely describe what it is he has actually done acting wise. The sideways glances to Shakes (played by Jason Patrick) across the court add tension, as defence lawyer Danny Snyder (an eccentric and bumbling Dustin Hoffman) moves in for questioning.

De Niro and Hoffman, sharing the screen for the first time here, take part in a calm volley of quietly spoken words, two old pros dominating the scene with ease. Bobby tells Snyder he was with John and Tommy that night at a basketball game, lying through his back teeth, but eerily for a priest, lying pretty damn well. Then they couldn't have killed the deceased then? asks Snyder. "Not unless they shot him from the blue seats at the garden," replies Bobby. "He was not shot by those boys," he adds. The priest has gone against everything he has ever believed in, but does so because he thinks he is doing the right thing, being loyal to the boys he watched grow up. Or perhaps it's out of fear? Either way, it packs a subtle punch and keeps you wondering just why he might have lied for them. Hoffman's role, though small, seems more noteworthy than it should be.

Dustin Hoffman is first and foremost an actor, a performer who takes whatever role interests him and gives it his all. However, since he is a known name and "bankable" on some level, reviewers and critics often seem more interested in the amount of money his films have taken, rather than how enjoyable they are. These days, the success of a picture is not in the artistic quality, but in the takings. In print, Mad City is by all means a failure. It cost 50 million dollars to finance yet made only 10 million back. Modern blockbuster fans would steer clear of a film that made a loss, for many choose their movies based on its ranking in the box office chart. But with Mad City they would be making a big mistake and missing out on an engaging, exciting and ultimately poignant thriller.

Dustin Hoffman plays Max Brackett, a local TV journo looking for a big scoop, and gets one when he finds himself in the middle a siege, involving fired security guard Sam Bailey (John Travolta) who is holding up a group of people hostage, including kids on a school trip, in the museum he once worked. Brackett, seeing he has access to a story that could restore his image as a hot reporter, begins to manipulate the situation, first making Bailey a working class hero, the little man fighting back against the system; then a villain, a bad guy created by the media through manipulation, misunderstandings and cynicism.

Mad City is an enthralling film, wonderfully directed by the French master Cost-Gravas and with a rich, full screenplay by Tom Matthews, and though it could easily have been cliché ridden and predictable, there are enough moralistic twists and turns to surprise the viewer at every turn. The acting, too, is sublime. Hoffman is very good as the corrupt, ruthlessly minded journalist, a man who will do anything for his chance at the big time but begins to develop a conscience when he sees what the media is really capable of, a realisation that becomes brutally blunt at the film's climax. The finest performance however, in my view at least, comes from John Travolta as the likeable, slightly slow and ultimately tragic Sam, a wide eyed innocent unaware of the seriousness of his actions and a helpless victim of a harsh, unforgiving, brainwashing media. The great Alan Alda delivers a fine effort too, but Hoffman and Travolta are the focus of the film and their interactions are the vital ingredients.

The reviews, however, were not so good, meaning that with bad notices and poor box office the film has gone down as a bomb; which seems unfair, given that all these years on it's a perfectly well made and executed mainstream rollercoaster, just as good or even better than the "best" commercial thrillers that emerged in the 1990s. Roger Ebert did not like the film much but admired Dustin's work, writing "Hoffman's performance is on target, and would have served a better screenplay."

Mad City is worthy of your time for a number of reasons; the satirical attacks on the media; the explosive ending including Hoffman's moralistic awakening; and of course the fine performances. Perhaps most important of all though is the fact it's so enjoyable, just as all good popcorn movies should be.

A year after their appearance together in Sleepers, Dustin Hoffman starred with Robert De Niro again in Barry Levinson's razor sharp Wag the Dog. With a truly excellent script by Hilary Henkin and David Mamet, the film boasts superb performances, snappy dialogue and political satire rarely if ever bettered on the silver screen.

In the film, De Niro plays Washington spin doctor Conrad Brean, who teams up with film producer Stanley Motss (Hoffman in a terrific Oscar nominated performance) in the build up to the election, to stage a fake war in order to distract the nation from the sex scandal involving the president. One gets the feeling that this may just have happened in real life, at least in a similar fashion, possibly numerous times in the murky world of U.S. politics.

The script is fast moving, full of quips, wit and hilarious one liners. In fact the whole film is extremely enjoyable and thought provoking, even if the tragic ending does jar somewhat with the general tone of the rest of the movie. In some ways though, it makes the sad finale pack an even greater punch, in light of the manic energy and humour bouncing back and forth between the glittering cast; the names of which include Dennis Leary, Anne Heche and Woody Harrelson, all brilliant in supporting roles. Like it or hate it, the final chapter also proves to the viewers what the film has been suggesting all along, that the government will do anything to cover up their mucky business. In the end, the consequences prove to be fatal for Hoffman's Stanley Motss. (Just in case any readers have not seen the movie, I will cease with any more spoilers.)

Hoffman provides all the energy and much of the light. Part of the reason that he is so strong in the role might be something to do with that fact that he based the character on his own father, rather than producer Robert Evans as some people would have you believe. For me it's the best performance of his from the 1990s and he hasn't matched it since in the following twenty odd years. It's a charismatic, egotistical character, delivered with such gusto and exuberance from Hoffman that it's one of the few more recent efforts which match the marvelous creations of his early films. In short, he should have won the Oscar. De Niro is brilliant too as the ponderous spin doctor, the red scarf and scruffy trilby hat the finishing touches of an already spot-on characterisation of a man who is always thinking. Again though, this is Hoffman's show, who dominates the film from his first appearance to his poignant last.

Hoffman has done some of his best work with Barry Levinson, from Rain Man to Sleepers and Wag the Dog. Sphere (1998), a science fiction thriller based on Michael Crichton's novel, was perhaps a little out of both men's comfort zone, yet Levinson still manages to make the film a genuinely creepy and unsettling piece of drama. Going more towards the psychological aspects of the genre, Sphere burrows its way into your head and unnerves you from the word go. Yet there is something about the whole thing that doesn't quite gel.

It follows a team of scientists who brave the depths of the Pacific Ocean to investigate the discovery of an alien spaceship on the surface. Staying at the nearby living facility Habitat, the scientists, including Dr Goodman (played by Dustin Hoffman) and Beth Halperin (Sharon Stone), discover that the craft is in fact American built and from the future. On board are various substances which the craft has collected from across the galaxy, including a fluid sphere which baffles them no end. Harry (Samuel L Jackson) enters the sphere and the crew come in contact with a being on the computer system called Jerry, presumed to be from the future. Forced to stay on board longer due to a devastating typhoon, things start to turn more bizarre and increasingly troublesome for the crew, as their worst fears become materialised before them.

In a time of complex sci-fi thrillers, with hits like Event Horizon and The Matrix at either side of it, Sphere seemed a little out of touch, its plot perhaps a little too convoluted and it failed at the box office. For a movie audience becoming increasingly more zombified by dumbed down pictures, I feel that Sphere suffered as a result of the shift in tastes. Had it had a smaller budget and aimed towards a different audience (not the blockbuster crowd), it could have made a profit. However, its bloated budget of 70 million dollars was not coming back.

Hoffman gives a suitably solid and reliable turn as the headstrong doctor and Sharon Stone is brilliant in a more intelligent, less sexually charged role. This is not a pot boiling, popcorn movie and perhaps that is why it has a slight jarring feel to it. It's big budget and full of effects, but its script doesn't support or enhance that format. In truth, it's a film that doesn't seem to know what it is, being lost between genres and styles somewhat awkwardly. That said, it's still quite an enjoyable and interesting ride, even if the critics disagreed.

Roger Ebert for once was able to nail what are essentially the film's most obvious flaws. "Sphere feels rushed," he wrote. "The screenplay uses lots of talk to conceal the fact that the story has never been grappled with. The effects and the sets are pitched at the level of made-for-TV fare. The only excellence is in the acting, and even then the screenplay puts the characters through so many U-turns that dramatic momentum is impossible."

Hoffman ended the decade with a curious cameo in Luc Besson's bold and daring cinematic telling of the life of Joan of Arc, which remains one of his least celebrated films. The film is not so much underrated, but completely ignored. Granted, this is no masterpiece, but it does paint an honest portrait of the French heroine and even though it's rather creaky in parts, it does feature some genuinely effective scenes. Besson's film admirably attempts to go for something new, capturing the emotional journey of Joan of Arc, rather than flatly recalling the events of her life as a more predictable narrative biopic would.

Milla Jovovich, largely known for her action roles in films like The Fifth Element and the Resident Evil franchise, delivers an honourable, awe inspiring performance, her screen presence dominating the film from the start, her dramatic range simply stunning. If there is one reason to watch the movie, above all else, do it for Jovovich's brave efforts. The film managed to make back its large 60 million budget, but fell victim to harsh reviews. Roger Ebert called it "a mess",

Dustin Hoffman has a small role towards the end, appearing as a mysterious, cloaked man in Joan of Arc's cell, certainly one of his weirdest parts. "Only Dustin Hoffman (normally a prince among hams)," wrote the Guardian, "manages to bring a little dignity to an otherwise ill-conceived role as Joan's testy 'conscience'. His limited screen time makes his appearance a minor note in a film dominated by an actress who has never received the credit she deserves.

It was a mixed decade for Hoffman, though it featured more ups than downs. He crept out of the 20th century in a cloak masking most of his iconic face, and re-appeared, three years later I might add, in a very different film environment. This was a new age of special effects and box office takings, things which were now very important in the modern film world, but totally alien to Hoffman's way of thinking about his craft. Dustin would never reach the brilliance of the 60s to the 90s, but he would keep working, rarely challenging himself and staying largely on the parameters of the supporting cast.

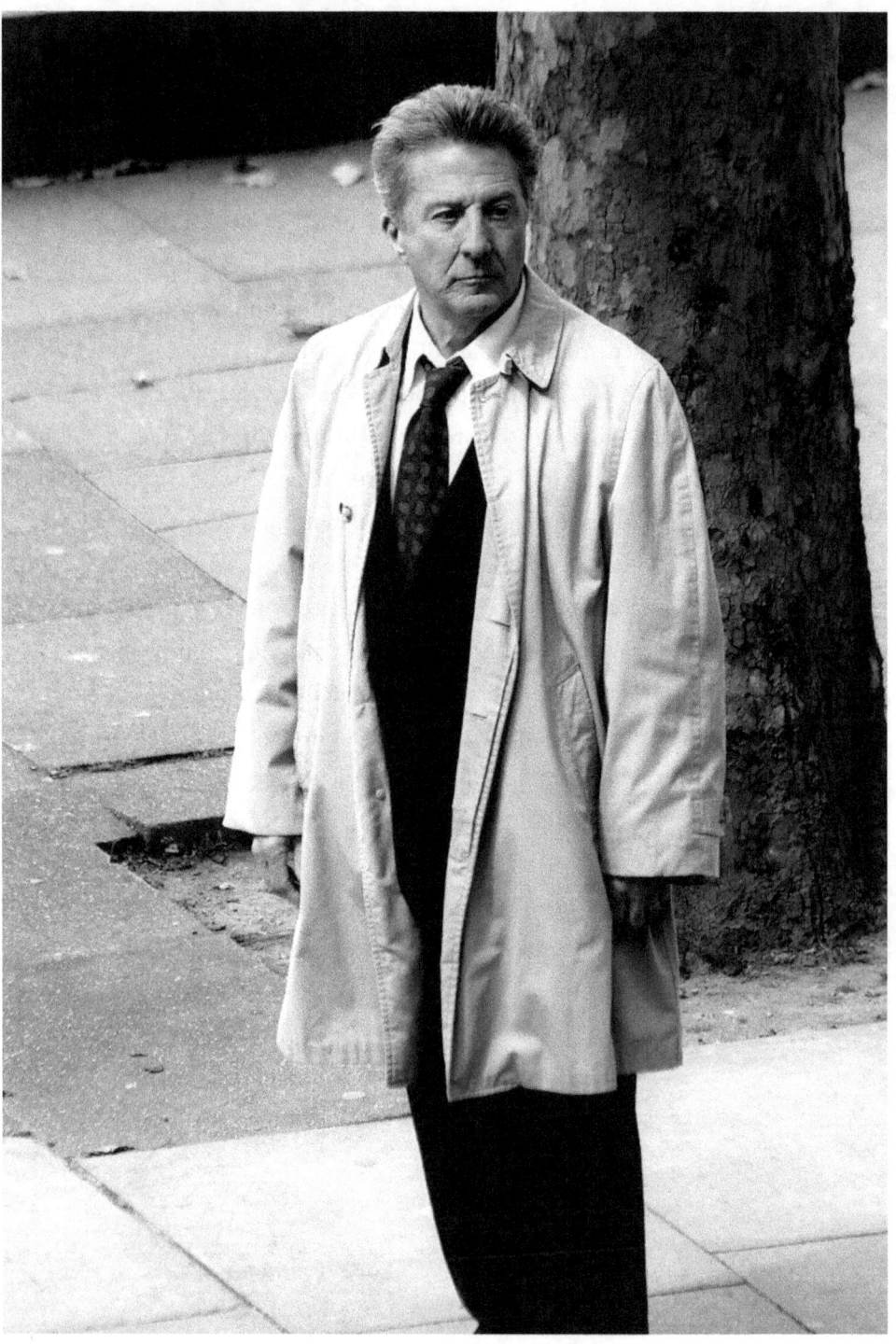

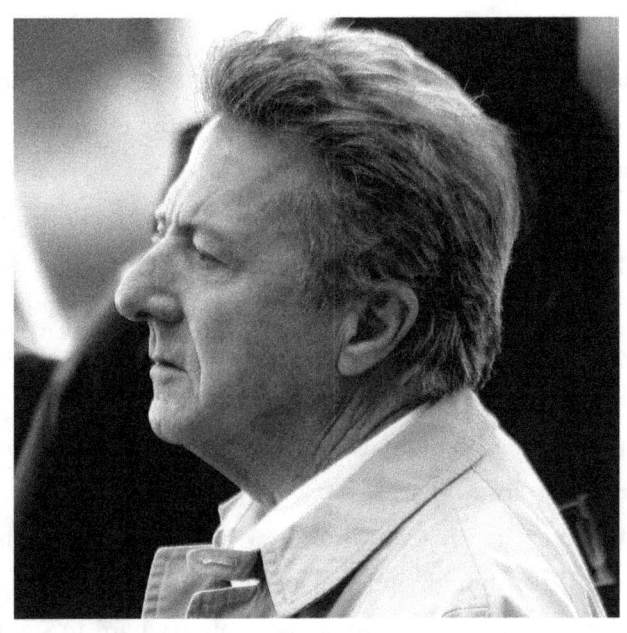

Last Chance Hoffman

Dustin Hoffman in Last Chance Harvey

In my view, 2008's Last Chance Harvey is the best Dustin Hoffman film of the 21st century. This may seem like an odd statement, considering the inconsequential lightness and sentimentality of the picture itself, but I have my reasons, which I believe are valid. Granted, on paper it's a standard romantic comedy, that doesn't really add to that much, with all its familiar ups and downs. What makes it special though is, again, its authenticity, the chemistry between its two leads and the naturalness they exude. It's familiar but not clichéd, safe but comforting, and it's made extra special by a charming script, unfussy direction and two wonderful performances.

To look at Hoffman's time in the 21st century, so far at least, is to see a formerly great iconic leading man taking small roles and the best of what he is offered. Rarely is he given the chance to flesh out a part, to see it through a rewarding journey to some kind of conclusion. That's not to say he's lost his ability to charm the viewer; not so, for he's as good as he can be, most of the time, in whatever he takes on. Take his first film of the new millennium for instance, the moving Moonlight Mile, in which Hoffman is subtly impressive as the grieving dad. It's a perfectly good effort. And to ignore the rest of his films from the past two decades is doing him an injustice, even if there are few gems in there.

He has even lent his voice to a few cartoons, like the three Kung Fu Panda films, though judging by one interview where he forgot which number film they were actually on, it's hard to say how "into" the movies Dustin really is. (Hoffman also wondered aloud to one interviewer what kind of animal his character in the franchise is.) He has also given small but noteworthy supporting turns in such films as I Heart Huckabees and Stranger Than Fiction. One performance of his which attracted serious criticism however, was his turn in Mr Magorium's Wonder Emporium (2007), in my view a charming film which suffered unfairly cynical reviews. His work in the two Meet the Parents sequels, as I said in my introduction, are among my least favourite of his performances, though he did add some class to films like The Cobbler, The Program and Boychoir. On top of that was his impressive directorial film debut, 2012's Quartet, a sizeable box office hit as well as a critical success. However, none of those pictures equal Last Chance Harvey.

In Last Chance Harvey, Hoffman plays Harvey Shine, a veteran jingle music writer who comes to London for his daughter's wedding, only to experience something of a lull when a number of unexpected things knock the wind out of his sails; firstly he is fired, he misses his plane back home, and most devastatingly of all, his daughter tells him she is going to have her step father give her away at the alter. Feeling sidelined, Harvey sulks around London until he meets Kate Walker, played by Emma Thompson, a stat collector for an airline who lives with her mother, and if she were to admit it, is helplessly lonely and love lorn. Though twenty years her senior, she strikes up a connection with Harvey which subtly and believably develops into a vague romance, though thankfully no wildly passionate fireworks fly. The film, though clichéd in its plot, development and pace outside of Hoffman and Thompson's scenes together, soars due to the appealing dynamics of its two stars, both unlikely romantic leads but a hundred times more watchable than the genre's usual breed of actors.

Dustin Hoffman has always been at his best when dealing with material he really cares about or has a personal attachment toward; Midnight Cowboy for instance was such a brave, bold performance, and came out so well, because he believed in the role so passionately and admitted to once having felt as unattractive and anonymous as Ratso; Kramer vs. Kramer, again, felt so real because for Hoffman it *was* real at the time; and Tootsie, another one of his best films, was so believable because he channelled all the frustrations from his own lean acting years into the desperation of his Michael Dorsey/Dorothy Michaels paradox. Last Chance Harvey is in a similar vein, and as Hoffman himself has said on numerous occasions, it was one of the most personal films of his career.

"I was thinking of Kramer vs. Kramer," he told Time Out in 2008. "That was 1979, so this is 30 years later, and that was about a guy getting a divorce, which I was in the middle of at the time. The same was true here – this film kind of explores the after-effects of what happens in Kramer, if I'm speaking personally. And in Kramer, I played closer to myself than ever. No limping or putting on accents. Emma Thompson and I realised we had something in common – we're both character actors, which means you're not good-looking enough to be the lead! So we said: Why don't we play this as close to ourselves as anything we've ever done?"

Director Joel Hopkins said he was a fan of both actors and was dying to work with them. "I love Emma Thompson and I love Dustin Hoffman and I thought: Why aren't I seeing them more? In Stranger Than Fiction, for instance, they were great but they were very peripheral characters. It was like: Why aren't they being used more? So, I thought that if I wrote a story for them, there's a chance they might do it. But it was never conscious. I was looking for characters for them and it turned out that because they are the ages they are, it became an older romance."

In terms of autobiographical elements, Last Chance Harvey is perhaps the closest Hoffman has gotten to himself in his whole on screen career. Consider firstly the fact that Harvey is a frustrated jazz pianist who took on commercials because it made him money, which mirrors Hoffman's own childhood experiences on the piano. Harvey is successful in a monetary capacity but there is no passion there. It may be lucrative but it's clear that Harvey has garnered very little pleasure from his career. Had he been a jazz pianist, he may have been poor, but he'd have been happy. Hoffman himself began his young life as a classical pianist, encouraged by his father to take the instrument up and take it somewhere. Hoffman though, had his eyes on being a jazz player. However, when he jammed with the real jazzers he realised he didn't have the ear or the talent for it. Alas, he quit the piano and through school took up acting, something he did not immediately fall in love with but grew to appreciate as a good outlet for his creativity. Still, at the back of his mind, Hoffman feels like a failed jazz pianist. Asked by an interviewer recently if he'd have swapped his film success for a career as a jazz pianist, he said yes without a moment's hesitation. Already, Hoffman has a lot in common with Harvey Shine.

There are other things which make Last Chance Harvey glow with authenticity. When Dustin said to Time Out that Harvey is Ted Kramer plus thirty years, one has to ponder on the consequences of a divorce and where that puts the people involved later in life. In Ted Kramer's case, as he keeps custody of his son, he will forever be a constant in Billy's world, a positive figure upon whom the son relies for stability and reassurance. Harvey though, seems to have been an emotional absentee, while her stepfather (played with quiet believability by James Brolin) has taken his place. Though Harvey thanks him for "being there" for his daughter in his wedding speech, there is a feeling that Harvey has been left behind, though the fact it seems to have been his own fault, partly, does lessen one's sympathy for him. Indeed, Hoffman does not cry out for our love and support, he plays the man with honesty. He is not perfect, but he's real, like all of Hoffman's finest creations.

There is something very warm and truthful about his developing romance with Kate too. The best moment, for me at least, comes at the end of the movie, when the connection has already been established. Kate is overcome with emotion and tells Harvey she cannot dive into a relationship, or even dip her toe in, because she knows there will be heartbreak and crushing disappointment somewhere down the line. She storms off and stands by the river, leaning off a railing and gazing at the water. Harvey however, does not go running after her like a younger man would; he gives her the moment, stands back and waits for her to calm down. In short, he gives her space, and it is when she turns, after ten or so seconds, and looks for Harvey in the crowd, that we know their relationship is going to work. He is mature and he knows the last thing Kate needs is a man invading her space. When they link arms and she removes her heels (making her the same size as Harvey, to which he quips "I think you're my kind of girl"), we believe it with sincerity that they are right for each other.

The key to the success of the part, and Hoffman's finest work, is its simplicity. Unnecessary dialogue and gestures were not what Ted Kramer and Harvey Shine needed. In one interview, Hoffman paraphrased the sculptor Henry Moore: "They say he was once asked, How do you do that big elephant, it must be so difficult, and he says, No, it's really not all that difficult, you just keep chipping away at what's not the elephant. And that's all you do, you just keep trying to get rid of that stuff that feels like detritus, it's dead skin. We don't know what we're going to wind up with, we just don't want to wind up with crap."

Last Chance Harvey was made on a tiny 5 million budget, and was a decent sized hit, making 32 million at the box office. Hoffman and Thompson had worked together on Stranger Than Fiction and were keen to butt heads again. When director Joel Hopkins gave them the permission to improvise and ensured Hoffman he would have input into the dialogue and flow of his scenes, he signed up immediately. With its naturalistic interactions and easy, fuss-free flow, it feels very much like a link in a chain, one which began with Kramer and ended up here, three decades on. There's a wholeness to it which ensures Last Chance Harvey requires repeated viewings. Indeed, it's the kind of film one picks out from the DVD collection every now and then for a reminder that integrity is possible to sustain in mainstream cinema.

"Em and I said can we play as close to ourselves as we've ever done," Hoffman said. "Our characters know we can survive unhappiness because we've built up those defences, but we're not sure we can survive happiness. That, to me, is the film, and on a daily basis I think we were both going to those areas in ourselves."

Reviews were mixed, though some were positive. However, many critics were bluntly honest about their personal conflicts with the material. The New York Times, though cynical in their review, did sum up rather well why such a potentially hackneyed idea came across so nicely, writing, "There's something irresistible about watching two people fall in love, even in contrived, sniffle- and sometimes gag-inducing films like Last Chance Harvey. I reluctantly gave in to this imperfect movie, despite the cornball dialogue, pedestrian filmmaking, some wincing physical comedy and Mr. Hoffman's habit of trying to win the audience over by simply staring at the camera with a hapless deadpan that says: Look at me, I'm still cute as a button, still cute as Benjamin in The Graduate, and I'm still kind of lost and still very much in need of your love."

The Telegraph took note of the stark contrast between Harvey and his other contemporary films. "Last Chance Harvey is a departure from Hoffman's recent work," they wrote, "for a start, it is a leading role, a two-hander with Emma Thompson. Whereas over the past few years he has opted for light-hearted cameos, where he can employ any number of tics and tricks (the lisp and wild hair of his 243-year-old toy owner in Mr Magorium's Wonder Emporium, the restless, endlessly coffee-drinking English professor in Stranger than Fiction, and the sparky hippie-throwback Bernie Focker in Meet the Fockers, to name but a few), in Last Chance Harvey he has stripped back the gimmicks and laid himself bare to play Harvey Shine, a divorced, lonely jingle writer, frustrated in all aspects of his life."

Roger Ebert called it "tremendously appealing love story surrounded by a movie not worthy of it. For Dustin Hoffman it provides a rare chance to play an ordinary guy. For Emma Thompson, there is an opportunity to use her gifts for tact and insecurity When Last Chance Harvey gets out of their way and leaves them alone to relate with each other, it's sort of magical."

It's a shame that Hoffman isn't offered more roles like this, fully realised characters with a complete arc within the film, rather than the supporting parts he tends to play these days. Harvey Shine, in my view at least, stands alongside his finest screen creations and in time will hopefully be recalled as fondly as the immortal icons of The Graduate, Midnight Cowboy, Straw Dogs, Marathon Man, Kramer Vs. Kramer, Tootsie and Rain Man. It's a sadly rare outing for Hoffman, for his part to be at the centre of a movie, which makes Last Chance Harvey even more of a unique treat.

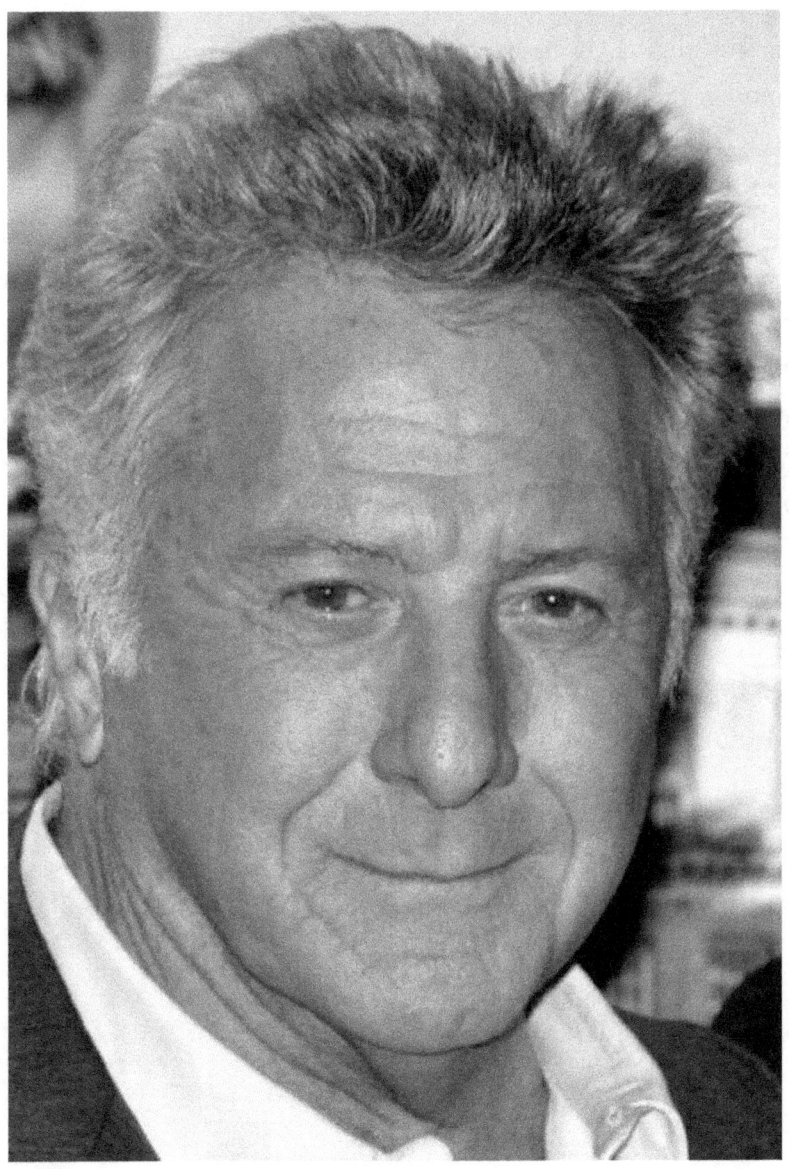

ABOUT CHRIS WADE

Chris Wade is a UK based writer, filmmaker and musician. As well as running the acclaimed music project Dodson and Fogg, he has written books on The Kinks, Picasso, Malcolm McDowell, Captain Beefheart, Robert De Niro and many others. He has also released audiobooks of his comedic fiction, such as Cutey and the Sofaguard, narrated by Rik Mayall. His other projects include Hound Dawg Magazine, for which he has interviewed such people as Sharon Stone, Donovan and Jethro Tull's Ian Anderson. His art films include The Apple Picker (accepted by Sydney World Film Festival, featuring Toyah Willcox and Nigel Planer), and he has made documentaries on Orson Welles and George Melly.

More info at his website: wisdomtwinsbooks.weebly.com